HOW TO CREATE THE PERFECT
Wedding

*L*et your journey to the altar begin with How to Create the Perfect Wedding, *the consummate guide to fashioning a ceremony filled with reflections of love. Overflowing with creative ideas, this 112-page handbook provides beautiful photos and imaginative suggestions for turning dreams into reality for the loving couple. Each section escorts you into a world of elegant, yet easy-to-craft, accessories designed to make each detail of the wedding especially memorable. We begin with inspiring shower themes that will surround the bride-to-be with the warm spirit of friendship. Our decorating options display nature's irrepressible romantic influence, with magnificent bouquets and tender floral embellishments that convey the secret language of love. And because a wedding is such a personal reflection of a couple's love and devotion, we propose six wonderful wedding themes that embrace both traditional and contemporary stylings. As you prepare for this most blessed day, allow us to help you make mementos and memories that will last a lifetime.*

Leisure Arts, Inc.
Little Rock, Arkansas

Contents

PRODUCTION STAFF
Technical: Beth Knife, Emily Ford
Editorial: Melia Lewis Mason, Tammi Williamson Bradley
Art: Brent Miller

Designs by Sandy Weyburn
Instructions tested by Sherri Mode and Janet Scholl

ISBN 1-57486-168-9
10 9 8 7 6 5 4 3 2 1

BRIDAL
Showers

A ceremony of sisterhood, the traditional shower honors the bride with warm wishes wrapped in ribbons of wisdom. Thoughtful gifts, while certainly appreciated, are almost secondary to the spirit of camaraderie and encouragement that permeates this feminine rite of passage. Surrounded by a loving circle of friends, the honoree blows a farewell kiss to her solitary life and bids welcome to her beloved and their future as husband and wife.

THE *Lingerie* SHOWER

With her romantic rendezvous only a short while away, you can heighten the bride-to-be's anticipation of those tender moments with a ceremony of femininity. In an atmosphere of elegant touches that celebrate the oneness of love, she will graciously receive delicate ensembles for her trousseau.

LARGE TOPIARY TREE
Approximately 25" tall

SUPPLIES
Square white lattice container (We
    used a 6¾" square container.)
Clay pot to fit inside container
Floral foam block for inside clay pot
Foam ball in proportion to square
    container (We used a 5" diameter
    foam ball.)
Lightweight colored satin
White poster board
1⅜ yds — 2"w white wired ribbon
1⅜ yds — 1½"w colored wired
    ribbon
Tree branch — approximately ½" in
    diameter and 21" long
8 large white silk roses
White silk azalea bush
2 bunches white silk Lily of the Valley
7" white dove
Spanish moss
9 large pearl sprays
¾ yd — 5mm strung pearls
Hot glue gun and glue sticks
    (optional)
Thick, clear-drying craft glue
Spray adhesive
Craft scissors or wire cutters
Knife to cut floral foam
Floral picks
Floral pins
Floral tape
Pebbles or small rocks

Please familiarize yourself with basic
techniques found in General
Instructions, pg. 108, before beginning
project. When a measurement for a
stem is given, that measurement
indicates the length of the stem from
the base of the flower or lowest leaf.

INSTRUCTIONS
1. Cut a piece of poster board and a piece of satin to fit inside each side of container.

2. Apply spray adhesive to one side of each piece of poster board. Matching wrong side of satin to adhesive-coated side of poster board, press satin pieces on poster board pieces. With covered sides facing outward, position poster board pieces inside container.

3. Place pebbles in bottom of clay pot. Using knife, cut foam to fit pot. Wedge smaller pieces of foam around large piece of foam, forming a firm base for topiary.

4. Insert one end of branch completely into center of foam in pot. Insert remaining end of branch approximately 3½" into center of foam ball. Remove branch from each piece of foam. Apply craft glue to 3" of each end of branch. Reinsert ends of branch into foam.

5. Place clay pot in container. Cover foam in pot with Spanish moss; secure moss with floral pins.

6. Follow Preparing Flowers And Greenery, pg. 108, to separate and trim all flowers and greenery to 2". Wrap stems of all flowers, greenery, and pearl sprays.

7. Randomly insert roses into foam ball; fill areas between roses with azaleas, greenery, and Lily of the Valley. Randomly insert pearl sprays into ball.

8. Tie white ribbon in a bow. Tie colored ribbon in a bow. Matching centers of bows, place colored bow on top of white bow; hand sew bows together. Refer to Assembling Arrangements, pg. 108, to insert floral pin through bows. Insert floral-pinned bows into foam ball.

9. Cut one 14" length and one 11" length of pearls. Fold each length in half to form a loop; secure ends by wrapping with thread. Refer to Assembling Arrangements, pg. 108, to place floral pins over thread on pearl loops. Insert floral-pinned pearl loops into foam behind bows.

10. Refer to Fig. 1 to fold and notch ends of all streamers.

Fig. 1

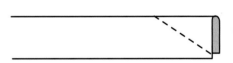

11. Place dove at base of tree in clay pot. Secure by placing floral pins over dove's claws and into foam.

SMALL TOPIARY TREE
Photo, page 6
Approximately 23" tall

SUPPLIES
    Square white wooden container (We
        used a 4½" square container.)
    Clay pot to fit inside container
    Floral foam block for inside clay pot
    Foam ball in proportion to square
        container (We used a 4" diameter
        foam ball.)
    1½ yds — ½"w colored striped
        ribbon
    Tree branch — approximately ½" in
        diameter and 21" long
    7 large colored silk roses
    9 colored silk rosebuds
    White silk azalea bush
    2 bunches white silk Lily of the Valley
    Spanish moss
    Hot glue gun and glue sticks
        (optional)
    Thick, clear-drying craft glue
    Craft scissors or wire cutters
    Knife to cut floral foam
    Floral picks
    Floral pins
    Floral tape
    Pebbles or small rocks

Please familiarize yourself with basic
techniques found in General
Instructions, pg. 108, before beginning
project. When a measurement for a
stem is given, that measurement
indicates the length of the stem from
the base of the flower or lowest leaf.

INSTRUCTIONS
1. Place pebbles in bottom of clay
    pot. Using knife, cut foam to fit
    pot. Wedge smaller pieces of
    foam around large piece of foam,
    forming a firm base for topiary.

2. Insert one end of branch
    completely into center of foam in
    pot. Insert remaining end of
    branch approximately 2½" into
    center of foam ball. Remove
    branch from each piece of foam.
    Apply craft glue to 2" of each end
    of branch. Reinsert ends of
    branch into foam pieces.

3. Place clay pot in container. Cover
    foam in pot with Spanish moss;
    secure moss with floral pins.

4. Follow Preparing Flowers And
    Greenery, pg. 108, to separate
    and trim all flowers and greenery
    to 2". Wrap stems of all flowers
    and greenery.

5. Insert several pieces of greenery
    into foam in pot. Randomly insert
    roses and rosebuds into foam
    ball; fill areas between roses and
    rosebuds with azaleas, greenery,
    and Lily of the Valley.

6. Cut ribbon in half. Tie each
    ribbon length in a bow. Matching
    centers of bows, place one bow
    on top of the other; hand sew
    bows together. Refer to
    Assembling Arrangements,
    pg. 108, to insert floral pin
    through bows. Insert floral-
    pinned bows into foam ball.

7. Refer to Fig. 2 to fold and notch
    ends of all streamers.

Fig. 2

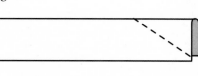

NUT CUP
Photo, page 6

SUPPLIES
    3¼"h white wire bird cage
    ½ yd — ½"w colored striped ribbon
    ½ yd — 1"w colored wired ribbon
    2 white silk azalea blossoms
    2" white mini dove
    Hot glue gun and glue sticks

INSTRUCTIONS
1. For wired ribbon bow, measure to
    a starting point 3½" from one end
    of ribbon and hold ribbon at this
    point between thumb and
    forefinger. For first loop, measure
    3" from starting point and fold
    ribbon to form a loop by matching
    starting point and second point.
    Measure 3" from second point
    and form loop by matching
    second point and third point.
    Measure 3" from third point and
    form loop by matching third point
    and fourth point. Leave 3½" of
    ribbon at the end of the third loop
    for streamer. Hand baste all loops
    and streamers together at the base
    of loops. Pull basting thread as
    tight as possible; secure and clip
    thread. Glue bow to top back of
    bird cage.

2. Thread striped ribbon through top front of bird cage; tie ribbon in a bow.

3. Refer to Fig. 3 to fold and notch ends of all streamers.

Fig. 3

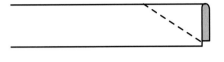

4. Glue azalea blossoms on top of cage between ribbon bows. Glue dove in place.

CORSAGE
Photo, page 6

SUPPLIES
8" diameter white Battenberg lace doily
¾ yd — 1"w colored wired ribbon
4 white silk azalea blossoms with leaves
5 white silk Lily of the Valley stems
1½"h white wire bird cage
Hot glue gun and glue sticks
Craft scissors or wire cutters
Corsage pin

INSTRUCTIONS
1. Fold doily as shown in Fig. 4. Place a pin at center and 2" from each side.

Fig. 4

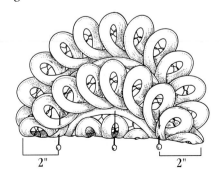

2. Refer to Fig. 5 to match each outside pin to center pin. Lower outside ends of doily should point downward. Hand sew folds in place along bottom edge.

Fig. 5

3. Trim azalea stems close to blossoms. Position azalea blossoms between doily layers; glue in place. Glue Lily of the Valley stems in place among azaleas.

4. For bow, measure to a starting point 5" from one end of ribbon and hold ribbon at this point between thumb and forefinger. For first loop, measure 2" from starting point and fold ribbon to form a loop by matching starting point and second point. Measure 2" from second point and form loop by matching second point and third point. Measure 2" from third point and form loop by matching third point and fourth point. Continue forming loops in this manner until you have six loops. Leave 6" of ribbon at the end of the sixth loop for streamer. Hand baste all loops and streamers together at the base of loops. Pull basting thread as tight as possible; secure and clip thread.

5. Glue bow to center of doily.

6. Glue bird cage to center of bow loops.

7. Refer to Fig. 6 to fold and notch ends of all streamers.

Fig. 6

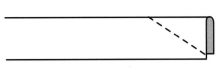

LAVENDER WAND
Photo, page 6

SUPPLIES
(*Note: Supplies are for making one lavender wand.*)
1 yd — 1"w colored wired ribbon
20 — 16" lavender stems
1 white silk Lily of the Valley stem
Hot glue gun and glue sticks
Craft scissors or wire cutters
18" length of 20 gauge floral wire
16½" x 12" x 2½" disposable aluminum foil pan
Kitchen utensil
Rubber band

INSTRUCTIONS
1. Cut floral wire in half. Use one length of wire to wrap lavender stems tightly together just below lavender buds. Trim excess wire.

2 Place lavender stems in foil pan. Place kitchen utensil on top of stem to hold under water. Fill pan with enough water to cover stems completely. Soak until stems are pliable (approximately 1-1½ hours).

3. Hold lavender with buds in your hand and stems pointing away from you. Gently bend stems back over wire, one at a time, until all stems are turned and form a cage encasing the lavender buds. Wrap loosely with rubber band below buds. Allow to dry completely.

4. Remove rubber band. Cut a 24" length of ribbon. Slip one end under two stems at top of wand as shown in Fig. 7. Fold ribbon back over raw edge and begin weaving ribbon in and out of stems as shown in Fig. 8. Continue weaving for 4".

Fig. 7

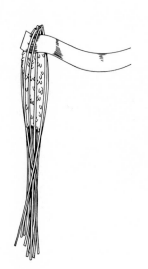

Fig. 8

5. Use remaining length of floral wire to wrap stems together 4" below top of wand; trim excess wire. Wrap loose end of weaving ribbon over wire; glue in place. Trim ribbon ends if necessary.

6. Glue Lily of the Valley in place.

7. Use remaining ribbon to tie a bow around wand stems.

8. Trim stems to desired length.

9. Refer to Fig. 9 to fold and notch ends of steamers.

Fig. 9

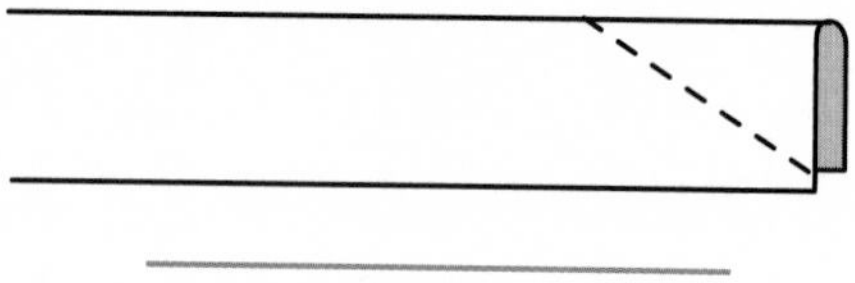

GIFT WRAP
Photo, page 6

SUPPLIES
(**Note**: Bow is approximately 7" diameter and is shown on an 8" square box.)
Colored pearlized wrapping paper
4 yds — 3"w white iridescent honeycomb ribbon
2 — 14mm pearls
5 large pearl sprays
1¼ yds — 5mm strung pearls
Hot glue gun and glue sticks
Double-stick tape

INSTRUCTIONS
1. Wrap box with pearlized paper and double-stick tape.

2. For bow, cut two 30" lengths, three 23" lengths, and two 7½" lengths of honeycomb ribbon.

3. Beginning at top center, wrap 30" lengths of ribbon around box; pinch ends of ribbon. Glue pinched ends to top center of box.

4. For streamers, pinch one end of each 7½" length of ribbon. Glue pinched ends to top center of box.

5. For bow loops, match short edges and fold one 23" length in half; lightly crease center. Unfold strip and lay it on a flat work surface. Fold each end to center, overlapping center crease by ½"; pinch all layers together at center. Glue loop to top center of box. Repeat with remaining lengths of ribbon, staggering loops as they are glued to box.

6. Glue 14mm pearls to center of bow. Glue pearl sprays between bow loops.

7. Cut one 12" length, one 14" length, and one 18" length of pearls. Fold each length in half to form a loop; secure ends by wrapping with thread. Glue loops to top of package under bow, draping loops over side of package.

8. Refer to Fig. 10 to fold and notch ends of streamers.

Fig. 10

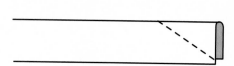

THE *Miscellaneous* SHOWER

It's only natural that starting a new life together will take "a little bit of this and a little bit of that." Allow us to propose a shower dedicated to the miscellaneous items that the love birds need to turn their house into a home. At this wonderfully personal celebration, bestow the bride with necessities to help her build a little love nest.

CENTERPIECE
Photo, page 11

SUPPLIES

Oval basket (We used a 6½"w x 8½"l x 3"h oval basket.)
Floral foam block to fit inside basket
Floral adhesive clay strip
14" tree branch with fork in center (14" from lower end to one fork tip, no larger than 1" diameter)
17" slim forked tree branch
1 colored silk snapdragon stem
3 tiny colored silk scilla blossoms
2 colored silk iris stems
2 silk stock stems (1 white, 1 colored)
3 colored silk wild roses
3 colored silk wild rosebuds
18" grass stem
2 — 7" fern fronds
1 bunch ivy with trailing stems
3 tiny artificial mushrooms
1½" colored mushroom bird
3" diameter nest
2½" diameter clay pot
1½" diameter clay pot
3 blue egg-shaped candies
Spanish moss
Floral sheet moss
Hot glue gun and glue sticks
Thick, clear-drying craft glue
Craft scissors or wire cutters
Knife to cut floral foam
Floral picks
Floral pins
Floral tape
2 — 18" lengths of 20 gauge floral wire

Please familiarize yourself with basic techniques found in General Instructions, pg. 108, before beginning project. When a measurement for a stem is given, that measurement indicates the length of the stem from the base of the flower or lowest leaf.

CUTTING CHART

1 iris stem	12½"
1 iris stem	9"
1 snapdragon stem	6"
1 white stock stem	6"
1 colored stock stem	4"
1 wild rose stem	5"
2 wild rose stems	3½"
2 fern fronds	2"
3 mushrooms	3½"

INSTRUCTIONS

1. Refer to Cutting Chart and follow Preparing Flowers And Greenery, pg. 108, to separate, trim, and wrap stems of fern fronds, mushrooms, and all flowers (except scilla and wild rosebuds). Trim scilla stems right below blossoms. Wrap grass stem with floral tape. Holding all stems of wild rosebuds together, join stems with floral tape; trim stems to 4".

2. Using knife, cut foam to fit basket. Place several strips of floral adhesive clay in bottom of basket. Place foam in basket, pushing foam into adhesive clay.

3. Cover foam in basket with sheet moss; secure moss with floral pins.

4. Wrap one length of floral wire around 14" tree branch below fork; twist wire ends together to form a stem. Trim stem to 2". Position tree branch across back one-third of basket with fork facing front of basket; insert wire stem into foam.

5. Position nest in front of branch. Insert floral pins through nest and into foam.

6. Thread remaining length of floral wire through hole in bottom of 2½" clay pot. Twist wire ends together on side of pot to form a stem *(Fig. 11)*. Trim stem to 2". Position pot on top of moss; insert wire stem into foam.

Fig. 11

7. Insert fern fronds at each side of basket.

8. Insert irises, snapdragon, and stock stems into foam. Insert 17" forked branch into foam between stock and snapdragon stems. Insert grass stem into foam close to rear iris.

9. Follow Preparing Flowers And Greenery, pg. 108, to separate and wrap ivy. Insert ivy into foam. Insert wild roses, wild rosebuds, and mushrooms into foam.

10. Hot glue 1½" pot on top of 2½" pot. Place a small amount of Spanish moss in each pot and in nest. Hot glue candies in nest. Hot glue bird in front of 2½" pot. Hot glue scilla to 2½" pot.

CORSAGE
Photo, page 11

SUPPLIES
2" diameter grapevine wreath
½ yd — 1"w colored wired ribbon
1 colored silk wild rosebud
2 tiny colored silk scilla blossoms
3 tiny colored silk scilla buds
3 tiny wired colored silk stamens
  for tendrils
3 tiny white silk stamens for eggs
  in nest
16 ivy leaves — assorted sizes
⅞" colored mushroom bird
Spanish moss
Hot glue gun and glue sticks
Craft scissors or wire cutters
Corsage pin

INSTRUCTIONS
1. Glue the 10 smallest ivy leaves to front of wreath.

2. Cut a 15" length of ribbon; tie in a bow. Glue bow to wreath at top center. Refer to Fig. 12 to fold and notch ribbon ends.

Fig. 12

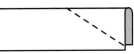

3. Glue bird to center of bow.

4. Glue remaining ivy leaves to wreath behind bird and between bow loops.

5. Trim rosebud and scilla stems right below buds or blossoms. Glue flowers among ivy leaves.

6. To form tendrils, twist each colored stamen wire around tapestry needle. Glue tendrils among ivy leaves.

7. Form a small amount of Spanish moss into a nest. Glue nest to inside bottom of wreath.

8. For eggs, trim wire stems from white stamens. Glue stamen into nest.

9. Matching short ends, fold remaining ribbon in half. Hand sew short ends together close to raw edges. Glue sewn portion of loop to back of wreath. Flatten loop against wreath. Insert corsage pin through ribbon.

GIFT WRAP
Photo, page 11

SUPPLIES
*(**Note**: Bow is approximately 9" wide and is shown on an 8½" x 11½" box.)*
Ivy print wrapping paper
2 colored silk mini stock stems
  (2 different colors)
4 colored silk wild rose blossoms
1 tiny colored silk scilla blossom
1 tiny colored silk scilla bud
17 — 32" lengths of natural straw
  raffia
Spanish moss
3" diameter bleached grapevine
  wreath
3 blue egg-shaped candies
Hot glue gun and glue sticks
Double-stick tape
Craft scissors or wire cutters

INSTRUCTIONS
1. Wrap box with ivy paper and double-stick tape.

2. Tie strands of raffia in a bow; glue bow to top of box.

3. To make nest, glue a small amount of Spanish moss in center of wreath; glue wreath to box below bow. Glue candies in nest.

4. Position all flowers behind and around bow, trimming stems as necessary; glue in place.

NUT CUP
Photo, page 11

SUPPLIES
2½" diameter clay pot
1 colored silk wild rosebud
2 tiny colored silk scilla blossoms
2 tiny wired colored silk stamens for
  tendrils
8 ivy leaves — assorted sizes
⅞" colored mushroom bird
Spanish moss
3" diameter grapevine wreath
3 blue egg-shaped candies
3 white egg-shaped candies
Hot glue gun and glue sticks
Craft scissors or wire cutters
Tissue paper
Size 16 tapestry needle

INSTRUCTIONS
1. Crumple tissue paper and place inside clay pot; glue in place. Form a small amount of Spanish moss into a nest. Glue nest on top of tissue paper.

2. Trim rosebud and scilla stems right below bud or blossoms.

3. To form tendrils, twist each stamen wire around tapestry needle. Position three ivy leaves, one scilla, and one stamen tendril at back rim of pot; glue in place. Place candies in nest. Glue bird to rim of pot.

4. Glue remaining ivy leaves, flowers, and stamen tendril to front of wreath. Insert bottom of pot through center of wreath.

NAPKIN RING
Photo, page 11

SUPPLIES
(**Note**: *Supplies are for making one napkin ring.*)

3" diameter bleached grapevine
    wreath
15" — 1"w colored wired ribbon
1 colored silk stock stem
1 colored silk wild rosebud
1 small ivy leaf
Hot glue gun and glue sticks
Craft scissors or wire cutters

INSTRUCTIONS
1. Trim mini stock stem below lowest blossom. Bend stem to conform to wreath; glue in place.

2. Tie ribbon in a bow; glue in place at base of stock stem.

3. Position rosebud and ivy leaf between flowers; glue in place.

4. Refer to Fig. 13 to fold and notch ends of streamers.

Fig. 13

LAVENDER WAND
Photo, page 11

SUPPLIES
(**Note**: *Supplies are for making one lavender wand.*)

1 yd — 1"w colored wired ribbon
20 — 16" lavender stems
Hot glue gun and glue sticks
Craft scissors or wire cutters
18" length of 20 gauge floral wire
16½" x 12" x 2½" disposable
    aluminum foil pan
Kitchen utensil
Rubber band

INSTRUCTIONS
1. Cut floral wire in half. Use one length of wire to wrap lavender stems tightly together just below lavender buds. Trim excess wire.

2. Place lavender stems in foil pan. Place kitchen utensil on top of stem to hold under water. Fill pan with enough water to cover stems completely. Soak until stems are pliable (approximately 1-1½ hours).

3. Hold lavender with buds in your hand and stems pointing away from you. Gently bend stems back over wire, one at a time, until all stems are turned and form a cage encasing the lavender buds. Wrap loosely with rubber band below buds. Allow to dry completely.

4. Remove rubber band. Cut a 24" length of ribbon. Slip one end under two stems at top of wand as shown in Fig. 14. Fold ribbon back over raw edge and begin weaving ribbon in and out of stems as shown in Fig. 15. Continue weaving for 4".

Fig. 14

Fig. 15

5. Use remaining length of floral wire to wrap stems together 4" below top of wand; trim excess wire. Wrap loose end of weaving ribbon over wire; glue in place. Trim ribbon ends if necessary.

6. Use remaining ribbon to tie a bow around wand stems.

7. Trim stems to desired length.

8. Refer to Fig. 16 to fold and notch ends of steamers.

Fig. 16

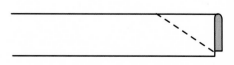

THE *Kitchen* SHOWER

Offering items of practicality elegantly situated amid decorative concepts, a kitchen shower blends all the necessary ingredients for an afternoon of fun. As cups of friendship are passed and filled again and again, guests will delight in our menu for success, which includes presentations from the bride's culinary theme followed by liberal servings of love and laughter.

CENTERPIECE
Photo, page 15

SUPPLIES
   White wire basket (We used a 12"w x 7"l x 5"h white wire basket.)
   White floral foam block to fit inside basket
   Floral adhesive clay strip
   White cotton fabric for attaching ruffle
   Printed chintz fabric for ruffle
   ⅝ yd — 1½"w colored striped wired ribbon for bow
   1½"w colored striped wired ribbon to tie around basket (allow for streamers)
   ⅞ yd — 1"w dark colored wired ribbon
   ½ yd — 1"w light colored wired ribbon
   ⅝ yd — 2"w white wired ribbon
   9 large white silk roses with white leaves
   2 small white silk roses
   1 bunch colored silk hydrangeas
   2 white plastic eggs on wire stems
   6 small kitchen utensils — (We used a 6¾" ladle, a 6" whisk, a 5½" strainer, a 5" nutmeg grater, a 7½" wooden spoon, and a 7¼" skimmer.)
   4 large white plastic utensils — (We used a spoon, a fork, a slotted spoon, and a set of measuring spoons.)
   2 — 18" square colored cloth napkins
   Hot glue gun and glue sticks
   Thick, clear-drying craft glue
   Craft scissors or wire cutters
   Knife to cut floral foam
   Floral picks
   White floral tape
   White poster board

Please familiarize yourself with basic techniques found in General Instructions, pg. 108, before beginning project. When a measurement for a stem is given, that measurement indicates the length of the stem from the base of the flower or lowest leaf.

INSTRUCTIONS
*(**Note**: Use a ½" seam allowance for all machine stitching.)*

1. To make ruffle, cut a 4" wide strip of fabric three times the outer dimension of basket (measure outer edges of basket; then triple measurement). This strip may be pieced if necessary.

2. Press both short edges of printed chintz ½" to wrong side. Matching **wrong** sides and long edges, fold length in half; press. Baste ½" and ¼" from long raw edges. Pull both basting threads until gathers measure outer dimension of basket. Secure and clip threads.

3. Cut two 3" wide strips of white fabric the outer dimension of basket plus 1". Matching right sides and raw edges, pin and baste gathered edge of ruffle to one long edge of one piece of white fabric with white fabric extending ½" beyond edge of ruffle on each end. Matching right sides and raw edges, place remaining piece of white fabric over ruffle; pin and stitch long raw edges together through all layers. Stitch short edges together on each end, being careful not to catch ruffle in stitching. Trim corners diagonally. Turn right side out and press, pressing white fabric away from ruffle.

4. Slipstitch short ends of ruffle strip together. This will be center back. With ruffle extending above edge of basket, hot glue white fabric to inside of basket. Cut poster board to fit bottom of basket. Insert poster board into bottom of basket.

5. Place several strips of floral adhesive clay on poster board in bottom of basket. Place foam inside basket, pushing foam into clay adhesive.

6. Follow Preparing Flowers And Greenery, pg. 108, to separate all flowers and leaves. Refer to Cutting Chart to trim all flowers and egg stems. Wrap stems of eggs, all flowers, and leaves with floral tape. Attach a floral pick to each plastic utensil and to four of the small utensils. Beginning at wire, wrap each pick with floral tape.

CUTTING CHART

3 large silk roses	5½"
1 large silk rose	5"
4 large silk roses	4"
1 large silk rose	3½"
2 small silk roses	3½"
3 hydrangeas	2½"
Egg stems	6"

7. Gather center of each napkin between fingers as shown in Fig. 17. Place floral pick alongside napkin with top of pick 5" above bottom point of napkin. Wrap wire around napkin and pick.

Fig. 17

8. Follow Assembling Arrangements, pg. 108, for the following: Insert large roses into foam in basket, placing taller roses near center and spacing roses around basket. Insert small roses into foam at center front of basket. Insert one egg into foam on each side of basket. Insert kitchen utensils with picks added and hydrangeas into foam. Insert one napkin into foam on each side of basket. Insert leaves into foam as desired.

9. For dark colored ribbon loops, measure to a starting point ½" from one end of ribbon and hold ribbon at this point between thumb and forefinger. For first loop, measure 7" from starting point and fold ribbon to form a loop by matching starting point and second point. Measure 7" from second point and form loop by matching second point and third point. Measure 7" from third point and form loop by matching third point and fourth point. Measure 7" from fourth

point and form loop by matching fourth point and fifth point. Leave ½" of ribbon at the end of the fourth loop. Hand baste all loops and streamers together at the base of loops. Pull basting thread as tight as possible; secure and clip thread. Wrap wire of floral pick around gathers. Covering wire, wrap pick with floral tape. Insert pick in basket.

10. For striped bow, measure to a starting point 1" from one end of striped ribbon and hold ribbon at this point between thumb and forefinger. For first loop, measure 5" from starting point and fold ribbon to form a loop by matching starting point and second point. Measure 5" from second point and form loop by matching second point and third point. Measure 5" from third point and form loop by matching third point and fourth point. Measure 5" from fourth point and form loop by matching fourth point and fifth point. Leave remaining ribbon at the end of the fourth loop for streamer. Hand baste all loops and streamers together at the base of loops. Pull basting thread as tight as possible; secure and clip thread. Repeat with white ribbon. Set bows aside.

11. Tie remaining 1½"w striped ribbon in a knot around basket, placing streamer ends at center front.

12. Tie three remaining small utensils together with 1"w light colored ribbon. Tie ribbon in a bow.

13. Hot glue striped bow and white bow to center front of basket. Hot glue small utensils to center of bows.

14. Refer to Fig. 18 to fold and notch ends of all streamers.

Fig. 18

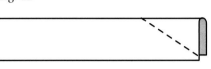

CORSAGE
Photo, page 15

SUPPLIES
7½" diameter white cutwork doily
5½" x 13" piece of printed chintz
1 yd — 1"w colored wired ribbon
3 small kitchen utensils (We used a 6" whisk, a 6" honey dipper, and a 5½" strainer.)
Hot glue gun and glue sticks
Corsage pin
Floral tape

INSTRUCTIONS
1. Arrange utensils; join handles together at center with floral tape.

2. Matching **wrong** sides, fold each long edge of printed chintz to center; press. Matching short edges, fold strip in half; lightly crease center. Unfold strip and lay it right side down on a flat work surface. Fold each short end to center, overlapping center crease by ½"; pin in place. Hand baste across center of fabric, stitching through all layers. Pull basting thread as tight as possible to gather fabric into bow; secure and clip thread.

3. Glue utensils to center of bow.

4. Hand baste along center of doily as shown in Fig. 19. Pull basting thread as tight as possible to gather doily; secure and clip thread. Glue doily behind fabric bow.

Fig. 19

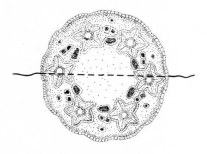

5. Cut a 16" length of ribbon. Tie ribbon in a knot around utensils just above fabric bow.

6. For bow, measure to a starting point 3" from one end of remaining ribbon and hold ribbon at this point between thumb and forefinger. For first loop, measure 2½" from starting point and fold ribbon to form a loop by matching starting point and second point. Measure 2½" from second point and form loop by matching second point and third point. Continue forming loops in this manner until you have four loops. Leave a 3" length of ribbon at the end of the fourth loop for streamer. Hand baste all loops and streamers together at the base of loops. Pull basting thread as tight as possible; secure and clip thread. Glue bow on top of knot around utensil handles.

7. Refer to Fig. 20 to fold and notch ends of all streamers.

Fig. 20

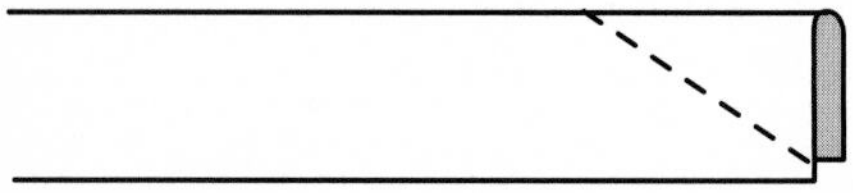

GIFT WRAP
Photo, page 15

SUPPLIES
Oval papier-mâché box (We used a 12½"l x 10"w x 6"h box.)
Printed chintz fabric to cover box
2⅝ yds — 1½"w colored striped wired ribbon
1½ yds — 1"w colored grosgrain ribbon
Grey spray primer
8 oz. white acrylic paint
1" foam paintbrush
2 colored champagne flutes
2 colored cloth napkins
2 — 6" white tapered candles
Square or heart-shaped white paper doily
White gift card
Spray adhesive
Thick, clear-drying craft glue
Double-stick tape
Tracing paper
Felt-tip pen
¼" eyelet kit
Awl

INSTRUCTIONS
1. Using #2 pencil, draw around box lid and bottom of box on tracing paper. Label each pattern. Cut traced patterns ¼" inside drawn line. Set patterns aside.

2. Follow manufacturer's instructions to spray interior and exterior of lid and box with primer. Repeat with additional coats as needed.

3. Using foam brush, paint interior and exterior of lid and box white. Repeat with additional coats as needed.

4. To determine size to cut fabric for covering side of lid, measure depth of lid and add ¼"; measure around outside of lid and add 1". Cut fabric the determined measurements.

5. Apply an even coat of spray adhesive to the wrong side of fabric. With one long edge of fabric ¼" below top edge of lid, smoothly press fabric to sides of lid; overlap ends 1". Fold and press fabric to inside of lid.

6. Using lid pattern, cut one fabric oval. Apply an even coat of spray adhesive to the wrong side of fabric oval. Centering fabric oval on lid, smoothly press fabric oval onto lid.

7. Repeat Step 4 to cut fabric to cover box sides.

8. Apply an even coat of spray adhesive to the wrong side of fabric. With one long edge of fabric ¼" above lower edge of box, smoothly press fabric to sides of box; overlap ends 1". Fold and press fabric to inside of box.

9. Repeat Step 6 using box bottom pattern to cut fabric oval.

10. Following manufacturer's instructions, attach eyelets to sides of box, using awl to punch holes.

11. Cut grosgrain ribbon in half. Thread one length through each eyelet on side of box; knot each end inside box.

12. Fold each napkin in half from top to bottom and again left to right.

13. Position napkins, candles, and champagne flutes on top of box. Tie in place with box ties. Use double-stick tape if necessary to hold items in place.

14. For bow, measure to a starting point 10" from one end of ribbon and hold ribbon at this point between thumb and forefinger. For first loop, measure 9" from starting point and fold ribbon to form a loop by matching starting point and second point. Measure 9" from second point and form loop by matching second point and third point. Continue forming loops in this manner until you have eight loops. Leave a 10" length of ribbon at the end of the fourth loop for streamer. Hand baste all loops and streamers together at the base of loops. Pull basting thread as tight as possible; secure and clip thread. Position bow on champagne glasses. Use double-stick tape to hold bow in place.

15. Cut corner or point of doily diagonally to fit long side of gift card. Glue cut edge of doily to wrong side of long edge of gift card. Write message on card with pen.

16. Refer to Fig. 21 to fold and notch ends of streamers.

Fig. 21

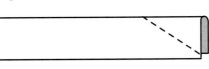

NUT CUP
Photo, page 15

SUPPLIES
2½"h colored glass candle holder
¾ yd — 1"w colored striped wired ribbon
9" diameter white crocheted edge doily
2 small colored silk blossoms
Hot glue gun and glue sticks
Double-stick tape
Craft scissors or wire cutters

INSTRUCTIONS
1. Leaving 1½" uncovered at center front, wrap a strip of double-stick tape around middle of candle holder.

2. Center candle holder on wrong side of doily.

3. Bring doily up around sides of candle holder. Press doily to tape. Cut a 9" length of ribbon. Tie ribbon tightly in a knot around candle holder to hold doily in place.

4. For bow, measure to a starting point 3" from one end of remaining length of ribbon and hold ribbon at this point between thumb and forefinger. For first loop, measure 3" from starting point and fold ribbon to form a loop by matching starting point and second point. Measure 3" from second point and form loop by matching second point and third point. Continue forming loops in this manner until you have four loops. Leave a 3" length of ribbon at the end of the fourth loop for streamer. Hand baste all loops and streamers together at the base of loops. Pull basting thread as tight as possible; secure and clip thread.

5. Glue bow to center front of doily.

6. Trim flower stems right below blossoms. Glue blossoms to center of bow.

7. Refer to Fig. 22 to fold and notch ends of all streamers.

Fig. 22

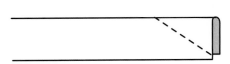

Floral ACCENTS

Whether a spray of lavish beauty or a single understated bud, flowers usher nature's quietly spoken language of love into the wedding ceremony. Communicating petal-soft sentiments, floral accents enhance the dreamlike wonder of the day while serving as expressions of the couple's delicately unfurling love. Beautifully swathed in ribbons and romance, your thoughtful touches are sure to plant seeds of happiness as love blooms on this special day.

PEW BOW

SUPPLIES

3 — 10" squares of white tulle
4½ yds — 2½"w white satin floral
   ribbon
⅓ yd — ¼"w white satin ribbon
1 large colored silk iris with bud
1 large white silk orchid
1 leaf bunch with small white berry
   clusters
4 fern fronds
3 — 17" grass stems
Hot glue gun and glue sticks
Craft scissors or wire cutters
Floral wire
3 floral picks
Floral tape
10" square of tracing paper

Please familiarize yourself with basic
techniques found in General
Instructions, pg. 108, before beginning
project. The measurements on the
Cutting Charts indicate the length of the
stem from the base of the flower or
lowest leaf.

CUTTING CHART

Iris stem	19"
Orchid stem	15"
2 leaves with one white berry cluster each	9"
4 fern fronds	8"

INSTRUCTIONS

1. Refer to Cutting Chart for
   measurements and follow
   Preparing Flowers and Greenery,
   pg. 108, to separate, lengthen,
   and wrap stems of iris, orchid,
   fern fronds, and two leaves from
   leaf bunch. Remaining leaves on
   bunch will be used as a group.
   Refer to Fig. 23 to hold iris and
   orchid together. Beginning below
   lowest blossom, join stems
   together with floral tape.

Fig. 23

2. Refer to Fig. 24 to position leaf
   bunch behind iris/orchid base.
   Join stems together with floral
   tape.

Fig. 24

3. Position remaining leaves with
   berry clusters below orchid. Join
   stems together with floral tape.

4. Position fern fronds and grass
   stems behind iris. Join stems
   together with floral tape. Carefully
   bend and arrange leaves, fern
   fronds, and grass stems around
   flowers as desired.

5. For hanger, cut a 10" length of
   floral wire; fold wire in half. Twist
   wire 1½" below fold to form a
   loop. With loop at back of flowers,
   wrap wire around flower stems.
   Leaving loop uncovered, wrap
   floral tape around stems to cover
   wire.

6. For bow, measure to a starting
   point 36" from one end of 2½"w
   ribbon and hold ribbon at this
   point between thumb and
   forefinger. For first loop, measure
   10" from starting point and fold
   ribbon to form a loop by matching
   starting point and second point.
   Measure 10" from second point
   and form loop by matching
   second point and third point.
   Continue forming loops in this
   manner until you have eight loops.
   For small loop, measure 5" from
   last point and fold loop as above.
   Leave a 39" length of ribbon at the
   end of small loop for streamer.
   Hand baste all loops and
   streamers together at the base of
   loops. Pull basting thread as tight
   as possible; secure and clip
   thread.

7. Tie ¼"w ribbon in a knot around
   gathering line of bow. To attach
   bow to arrangement, thread ¼"w
   ribbon on bow through flower
   stems; tie in a knot at back of
   arrangement. Glue knot in place.

8. Pull small loop to front of bow to
   cover ¼"w ribbon, glue in place.
   Trim ribbon ends as desired.

9. For circle, fold tracing paper in half and place folded edge along heavy solid line on pattern (shown in grey on page 112). Use pencil to trace pattern on tracing paper; cut out traced pattern. Unfold pattern and lay it flat. Use pattern to cut three tulle circles.

10. To form pouf, gather center of one tulle circle between fingers; wrap gathers with thread. Wrap wire of pick around pouf gathers *(Fig. 25)*. Covering wire, wrap pick with floral tape. Repeat with remaining tulle circles. Glue picks to flower stems.

Fig. 25

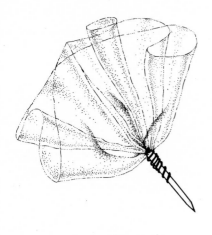

TOASTING GLASSES

SUPPLIES
2 champagne glasses
2 — 6" x 9" pieces of dotted tulle
1 yd — ¼"w white satin ribbon
½ yd — ¼"w colored satin ribbon
⅝ yd — ⅛"w white satin ribbon
⅓ yd — ⅛"w colored satin ribbon
1 pkg 3mm pearl beads
2 colored ribbon roses
   (approximately ⅞" dia.)
6 pearl loop sprays
Jewel glue
Double-stick tape

INSTRUCTIONS
1. Machine stitch ¼"w white ribbon to both long edges of each length of tulle.

2. Glue 3mm pearls to right side of each length of tulle, leaving ¾" unbeaded along short edges.

3. Matching short ends, fold one length of tulle in half; lightly crease center. Unfold tulle and place wrong side up on a flat work surface. Fold each short end to center, overlapping center crease by ½"; pin in place. Machine baste across center, stitching through all layers. Pull basting thread tightly to gather tulle into bow; secure and clip thread. Repeat with remaining length of tulle.

4. Cut two 10" lengths of ⅛"w white ribbon; tie one length in a knot around center of each bow.

5. To make ribbon loops, cut ¼"w colored ribbon in half. Measure to a starting point 2" from one end of one ribbon length and hold ribbon at this point between thumb and forefinger. For first loop, measure 2" from starting point and fold ribbon to form a loop by matching starting point and second point. Measure 1½" from second point and form loop by matching second point and third point. Leave a 2" length of ribbon at the end of second loop for streamer. Tack all loops and streamers together at the base of loops. Repeat with remaining ribbon length.

6. Cut ⅛"w colored ribbon in half. Matching short edges, fold one ribbon length in half. Tack both layers together ¾" from fold. Repeat with remaining ribbon length.

7. Hand sew one ¼"w and one ⅛"w ribbon loop together; hand sew loops to center of a bow. Hand sew one ribbon rose to bow on top of loops; trim ribbon ends as desired. Repeat with remaining ribbon loops, ribbon rose, and bow.

8. Wrap a piece of double-stick tape around top of each glass stem. Trim stems of pearl loop sprays to ½". Press stems of three pearl loop sprays to tape on each glass.

9. Placing ribbon over pearl spray stems, tie one bow to each glass with ⅛"w white ribbon ties.

GUEST BOOK HOLDER

SUPPLIES
*(**Note**: Guest book holder is sized for an 8½" x 6¼" guest book.)*
½ yd — 44/45"w white satin
½ yd — 44/45"w fleece
14" x 18" piece of foamcore board
14" x 15" piece of white poster board
1⅛ yds — 2¼"w colored satin ribbon
1 yd — ⅜"w colored satin ribbon
2 white silk lilac stems with leaves
1 large colored silk rose with leaf
   clusters
1 colored silk rosebud
Hot glue gun and glue sticks
Thick, clear-drying craft glue
Fray Check™
Craft scissors or wire cutters
Craft knife
Floral tape
Tracing paper
Emery board

Please familiarize yourself with basic techniques found in General Instructions, pg. 108, before beginning project.

INSTRUCTIONS

1. For book holder and ledge, fold tracing paper in half and place folded edge along heavy solid line on patterns (shown in grey on page 111). Use pencil to trace patterns on tracing paper, matching dashed lines of book holder patterns to extend pattern; cut out traced patterns. Draw around patterns on foamcore board. Using craft knife, cut foamcore along drawn lines. Smooth any rough edges with emery board.

2. Draw around book holder pattern on poster board and fleece. Cut poster board shape ⅛" inside drawn lines. Cut fleece along drawn lines.

3. Draw around foamcore shapes and poster board shape on satin. Cut each satin shape ½" outside drawn lines. Apply Fray Check™ to raw edges of all satin pieces; allow to dry.

4. Use craft glue to attach fleece shapes to corresponding foamcore shapes.

5. With fleece side down, center foamcore book holder shape on wrong side of satin. Wrap satin over foamcore shape, folding and pleating satin at corners as necessary; glue in place with craft glue. Secure with pins until glue is dry.

6. Repeat Step 5 to cover foamcore ledge.

7. Center poster board shape on wrong side of corresponding satin piece. Wrap edges of satin over poster board; glue in place with craft glue.

8. Matching wrong sides, center covered poster board on covered foamcore; glue in place with craft glue.

9. Matching lower edges, use craft glue to glue ledge to bottom of book holder.

10. Refer to Preparing Flowers and Greenery, pg. 108, to trim leaves from lilac stems; trim lilac stems to 3". Wrap stems of lilacs with floral tape. Set leaves aside to be used later.

11. Place lilacs together end to end, overlapping stems 2½" *(Fig. 26)*. Wrap overlapped stems with floral tape.

Fig. 26

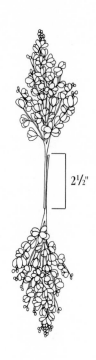

2½"

12. Follow Preparing Flowers and Greenery, pg. 108, to remove leaves and trim rose stem to 3" and rosebud stem to 4". Wrap each stem with floral tape. Set leaves aside to be used later.

13. Position rose and rosebud as shown in Fig. 27. Join stems together with floral tape.

Fig. 27

14. Carefully bend and arrange rose, rosebud, and lilacs to fit top of covered book holder. Hot glue flower stems to book holder.

15. For ribbon loops, cut three 7" lengths of 2¼"w ribbon. Matching short edges, fold one length in half. Baste ¼" from short edges. Tightly gather ends *(Fig. 28)*; secure and clip thread. Repeat with remaining lengths of ribbon.

Fig. 28

16. Hot glue ribbon loops to book holder.

17. For streamers, cut two 9" lengths of 2¼"w ribbon. Refer to Fig. 29 to fold and notch ribbon ends. Hot glue streamers to book holder.

Fig. 29

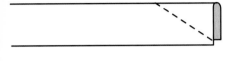

18. Hot glue leaves between flowers and ribbon loops as desired.

19. For bookmark and pen tie, match short edges and fold ⅜"w ribbon length in half; tie an overhand knot close to fold. Hot glue ribbon knot under rose.

CAKE KNIFE
Photo, page 25

SUPPLIES
Cake knife
6" x 9" piece of dotted tulle
1 yd — ⅝"w white satin ribbon
⅞ yd — ¼"w white satin ribbon
1 yd — ¼"w colored satin ribbon
10" — ⅛"w white satin ribbon
¾ yd — ⅛"w colored satin ribbon
1 pkg 3mm pearl beads
Colored ribbon rose (approximately ⅞" dia.)
2 pearl sprays
Jewel glue

INSTRUCTIONS
1. Machine stitch ¼"w white ribbon to both long edges of tulle.

2. Glue 3mm pearls to right side of tulle, leaving ¾" unbeaded along short edges.

3. Matching short ends, fold tulle in half; lightly crease center. Unfold tulle and place wrong side up on a flat work surface. Fold each short end to center, overlapping center crease by ½"; pin in place. Machine baste across center, stitching through all layers. Pull basting thread tightly to gather tulle into bow; secure and clip thread.

4. Tie ⅛"w white ribbon in a knot around center of bow.

5. Matching short edges, fold ⅝"w white ribbon in half. Hand sew ribbon fold to back of tulle bow below ⅛"w ribbon.

6. Glue pearl sprays to center of tulle bow.

7. To make ribbon loops, measure to a starting point 15½" from one end of ¼"w colored ribbon and hold ribbon at this point between thumb and forefinger. For first loop, measure 1½" from starting point and fold ribbon to form a loop by matching starting point and second point. Measure 2" from second point and form loop by matching second point and third point. Leave a 17" length of ribbon at the end of second loop for streamer. Tack all loops and streamers together at the base of loops.

8. For additional ribbon loops, measure to a starting point 11" from one end of ⅛"w colored ribbon and hold ribbon at this point between thumb and forefinger. For first loop, measure 1½" from starting point and fold ribbon to form a loop by matching starting point and second point. Measure 1½" from second point and form loop by matching second point and third point.

Measure 1½" from third point and form loop by matching third point and fourth point. Leave an 11" length of ribbon at the end of third loop for streamer. Tack all loops and streamers together at the base of loops.

9. Hand sew both ribbon loops to center of bow. Hand sew ribbon rose to bow on top of loops. Trim ribbon ends as desired.

10. Tie bow to knife with ⅛"w white ribbon ties.

TABLE CENTERPIECE
Photo, page 28

SUPPLIES
1¼ yds — 6"w colored tulle
2½ yds — 2¾"w white moiré wired ribbon
2⅝ yds — 1¾"w white and colored striped ribbon
2½ yds — 1½"w colored wired ribbon
1¼ yds — ¼"w white satin ribbon
18" ficus leaf spray
4 colored silk tiger lilies with one bud each
1 colored silk tiger lily
2 white silk tiger lilies with one bud each
4 white silk tiger lilies
2 colored fluffy filler sprays
4 white silk Lily of the Valley stems
1 colored silk apple blossom bunch
Hot glue gun and glue sticks
Craft scissors or wire cutters
2 floral picks
Floral tape

Please familiarize yourself with basic techniques found in General Instructions, pg. 108, before beginning project.

The measurements on the Cutting Charts indicate the length of the stem from the base of the flower or lowest leaf.

CUTTING CHART

1 colored tiger lily with bud	16"
1 colored tiger lily	16"
1 colored tiger lily with bud	15"
1 colored tiger lily with bud	14"
1 colored tiger lily with bud	13"
1 white tiger lily with bud	14"
1 white tiger lily with bud	13"
1 white tiger lily	10"
2 white tiger lilies	9"
1 white tiger lily	8"
2 fluffy filler sprays	15"
4 white Lily of the Valley stems	6"

INSTRUCTIONS

1. Refer to Cutting Chart for measurements and follow Preparing Flowers and Greenery, pg. 108, to separate, lengthen, and wrap stems of all flowers except apple blossom bunch. Holding all stems of Lily of the Valley together, join stems together with floral tape. Set

Lily of the Valley aside. Position colored lilies in front of ficus leaf spray as shown in Fig. 30. Beginning below lowest blossom, join all stems together with floral tape.

Fig. 30

2. Refer to Fig. 31 to position white lilies. Beginning below lowest blossom, join stems together with floral tape.

Fig. 31

3. Position filler sprays on sides of arrangement. Join stems together with floral tape.

4. Position Lily of the Valley below white lilies. Join stems together with floral tape.

5. For white moiré bow, measure to a starting point 25" from one end of ribbon and hold ribbon at this point between thumb and forefinger. For first loop, measure 10" from starting point and fold ribbon to form a loop by matching starting point and second point. Measure 10" from second point and form loop by matching second point and third point. Measure 9" from third point and form loop by matching third point and fourth point. Measure 9" from fourth point and form loop by matching fourth point and fifth point. Leave a 25" length of ribbon at the end of fourth loop for streamer. Hand baste all loops and streamers together at the base of loops. Pull basting thread as tight as possible; secure and clip thread. Tie ¼"w ribbon in a knot around gathering line of bow.

6. For striped bow, measure to a starting point 28" from one end of ribbon and hold ribbon at this point between thumb and forefinger. For first loop, measure 9" from starting point and fold ribbon to form a loop by matching starting point and second point. Measure 9" from second point and form loop by matching second point and third point. Measure 8½" from third point and form loop by matching third point and fourth point. Measure 8½" from fourth point and form loop by matching fourth point and fifth point. Leave a 28" length of ribbon at the end of fourth loop for streamer. Hand baste all loops and streamers together at the base of loops. Pull basting thread as tight as possible; secure and clip thread.

7. Place striped bow on top of white bow, bringing striped streamers between loops of white bow; hand sew striped bow in place.

8. For colored bow, measure to a starting point 28" from one end of ribbon and hold ribbon at this point between thumb and forefinger. For first loop, measure 9" from starting point and fold ribbon to form a loop by matching starting point and second point. Measure 9" from second point and form loop by matching second point and third point. Continue forming loops in this manner until you have four loops. Leave a 25" length of ribbon at the end of fourth loop for streamer. Hand baste all loops and streamers together at the base of loops. Pull basting thread as tight as possible; secure and clip thread. Matching centers, glue colored bow on top of striped bow.

9. Trim stems on apple blossom bunch close to where all stems are taped together. Glue apple blossom bunch to center of white bow.

10. Fold each colored ribbon streamer to form a small loop that will cover apple blossom stems. Glue ribbon loops in place.

11. To attach bows to arrangement, thread ¼"w ribbon on bows through flower stems; tie in a knot at back of arrangement. Glue knot in place.

12. For double tulle loops, cut four 11" lengths of tulle. Matching short edges, fold each length in half. Matching short edges, stack two loops together. Hand baste through all thicknesses ¼" from short raw edges. Pull basting thread as tight as possible; secure and clip thread. Place floral pick alongside loops ¾" above gathering line. Wrap wire of pick around loops. Covering wire, wrap pick with floral tape. Repeat with remaining loops. Glue picks to floral stems.

13. Refer to Fig. 32, to fold and notch all ribbon ends.

Fig. 32

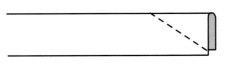

CANDELABRA SPRAY
Photo, page 31

SUPPLIES
4¾ yds — 2½"w satin florist ribbon
⅓ yd — ¼"w satin ribbon
2 — 18" ficus leaf sprays
6 silk freesia stems
2 large silk roses
3 silk Lily of the Nile sprays
2 silk stephanotis stems
1 bunch ivy
Hot glue gun and glue sticks
Craft scissors or wire cutters
Floral wire
Floral tape

Please familiarize yourself with basic techniques found in General Instructions, pg. 108, before beginning project. The measurements on the Cutting Charts indicate the length of the stem from the base of the flower or lowest leaf.

CUTTING CHART

2 Freesia stems	12"
2 Freesia stems	10"
1 Freesia stem	9"
1 Freesia stem	8"
2 Rose stems	4"
3 Lily of the Nile sprays	2" (begin measuring at point where all stems are joined together)
2 Stephanotis stems	3"
2 Ivy clusters	5½"

INSTRUCTIONS

1. Refer to Cutting Chart for measurements and follow Preparing Flowers and Greenery, pg. 108, to separate, lengthen, and wrap stems of freesia, roses, stephanotis, and ivy. Do **not** separate Lily of the Nile sprays; wrap stems.

2. Wrap stems of ficus leaf sprays. Place sprays together end to end, overlapping stems 4" *(Fig. 33)*. Wrap overlapped stems with floral tape.

Fig. 33

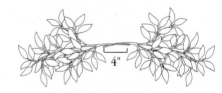

3. Position freesia stems on ficus leaf base *(Fig. 34)*. Join stems together with floral tape.

Fig. 34

4. Position rose stems on ficus leaf/freesia base *(Fig. 35)*. Join stems together with floral tape.

Fig. 35

5. For hanger, cut a 10" length of floral wire; fold wire in half. Twist wire ¾" below fold to form a loop. With loop at back of flowers, wrap wire around center of flower stems. Leaving loop uncovered, wrap floral tape around stems to cover wire.

6. Position Lily of the Nile sprays between roses. Join each spray to arrangement by wrapping with floral tape. Carefully bend and arrange flowers as desired.

7. Position ivy and stephanotis stems in arrangement. Join each stem to arrangement by wrapping with floral tape.

8. For bow, measure to a starting point 40" from one end of 2½"w ribbon and hold ribbon at this point between thumb and forefinger. For first loop, measure 10" from starting point and fold ribbon to form a loop by matching starting point and second point. Measure 10" from second point and form loop by matching second point and third point. Continue forming loops in this manner until you have eight loops. For small loop, measure 6" from last point and fold loop as above. Leave a 43" length of ribbon at the end of small loop for streamer. Hand baste all loops and streamers together at the base of loops. Pull basting thread as tight as possible; secure and clip thread.

9. Tie ¼"w ribbon in a knot around gathering line of bow. To attach bow to arrangement, thread ¼"w ribbon on bow through flower stems; tie in a knot at back of arrangement. Glue knot in place.

10. Pull small loop to front of bow to cover ¼"w ribbon; glue in place. Trim ribbon ends as desired.

WEDDING
Mementos

Wedding keepsakes tenderly preserve memories from each endearing event surrounding the ceremony. Petals from pressed flowers, invitations to showers, and photo albums carefully chronicle this joyous journey and become mementos the happy couple will cherish for a lifetime. Because the day embraces family and special friends, appropriate tokens of appreciation should be bestowed upon the bridal party as well. Such handcrafted sentiments share the blissfulness of the day with all.

A Bridal Shower

COVERED PHOTO ALBUM

SUPPLIES

*(**Note**: Other size albums may have different fabric and trim requirements.)*

10"w x 11½"h photo album with a
    2" spine
¾ yd — 44/45"w satin
2 — 22½" x 11½" pieces of fleece
Linen cutwork hand towel
¾ yd — ¼"w satin ribbon for ties
1 double tassel satin cord
½ yd — 5mm string pearls
1 pkg 5mm half-round pearls
1 pkg 3mm pearls
Thick, clear-drying craft glue
2 — 8¼" x 11¼" pieces of white
    poster board

INSTRUCTIONS

1. Remove pages from album.

2. Cut two strips of satin 2½" x 11½". Glue one long edge of each satin strip ¼" under inside metal spine of album. Glue remaining edges of satin strips to album.

3. Hand baste pieces of fleece together along outer edges. Glue fleece to outside of album.

4. Cut a piece of satin 26" x 15". With fleece side down, center album on wrong side of satin. Glue satin to corners on inside of album, folding and pleating as necessary; secure with pins until glue is dry.

5. Apply glue to inside bottom edge of album. Turn satin at bottom of album ¼" to wrong side for 4" in center *(Fig. 36)*. Insert folded satin under spine of album. Glue remaining satin to bottom edge of album, checking frequently to be sure satin is smooth and taut; secure with pins until glue is dry. Repeat with top edge of album.

Fig. 36

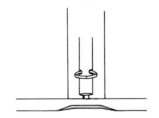

6. Glue satin to remaining inside edges of album, being sure satin is taut and smooth; secure with pins until glue is dry.

7. Matching short edges, fold hand towel in half; cut along fold line. Place cutwork end of towel on album cover. Glue top and right edges of towel to inside of album. Glue left edge of towel to spine of album.

8. Cut ¼"w ribbon in half. Glue one length of ribbon to center of each cover on inside, leaving approximately 10" of ribbon free.

9. Cut two pieces of satin 10¼" x 13". Center one poster board shape on wrong side of one piece of satin. Wrap satin over corners of poster board shape; glue in place. Glue remaining satin edges to poster board shape. Repeat with remaining poster board shape and satin piece.

10. Glue wrong sides of covered poster board shapes to inside of album.

INSTRUCTIONS

1. To determine size to cut fleece for lining inside of box, measure inside depth of box and around inside of box. Cut fleece determined size.

2. Place a strip of double-stick tape around inside of box ¼" below top edge. Matching one long edge of fleece to top edge of box, press fleece to tape.

3. To line inside of box, cut a 6" x 24" bias strip of satin. Place a strip of double-stick tape around outside of box 2" below top edge. Beginning at center back and with right side of satin strip facing out, position one long edge of satin strip around box over tape *(Fig. 37)*. Trim short edge of satin strip 2" beyond center back. Fold unattached short edge 1" to wrong side; pin in place. Fold satin strip to inside of box; glue raw edges to inside bottom of box.

Fig. 37

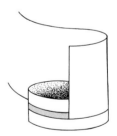

4. Draw around box bottom two times and box top once on poster board. Lightly label box bottoms and top. Cut box bottoms and top along drawn lines. Trim one box bottom to fit inside box. Trim box top to fit inside box lid.

11. Glue strung pearls along edge of towel. Randomly glue half-round pearls and 3mm pearls to towel.

12. For bow, measure to a starting point 6½" from end of one tassel and hold cord at this point between thumb and forefinger. For first loop, measure 4½" from starting point and fold cord to form a loop by matching starting point and second point. Measure 4½" from second point and form loop by matching second point and third point. Continue making loops in this manner until you have four loops. Leave remaining length of cord for streamer. Hand sew all loops and streamers together at the base of loops; secure and clip thread. Glue bow to album.

SATIN COVERED BOX

SUPPLIES

7" oval Shaker box
⅞ yd — 44/45"w satin
⅜ yd — 44/45"w fleece
2 — 7" x 6" pieces of batting
¼ yd — 6"w tulle
¾ yd — ⅝"w satin ribbon
⅝ yd — twisted satin cord
Double tassel satin cord
Small mushroom bird
Silk flower spray with leaves
Fray Check™
Thick, clear-drying craft glue
Double-stick tape
Craft scissors or wire cutters
1 sheet white poster board

5. Draw around each poster board box bottom and top on fleece. Cut fleece along drawn lines. Glue fleece to each poster board box bottom and box top.

6. Draw around each poster board box bottom and top on wrong side of satin. Cut satin 1" outside drawn lines. Hand baste around each satin box bottom and top ¼" from raw edges.

7. Center fleece side of one poster board box bottom on wrong side of corresponding satin box bottom. Pull basting thread to draw satin up over edges of poster board; secure and clip thread. Glue edges of satin in place. Repeat with remaining poster board and satin box bottom and top.

8. Apply glue to inside bottom of box. Insert smaller satin-covered box bottom into box.

9. To determine size to cut poster board for covering outside of box, measure depth of outside of box and subtract ½". Measure around outside of box and add 1". Cut poster board determined size.

10. Draw around poster board shape on wrong side of satin. Cut satin 1" outside drawn lines.

11. Center poster board shape on wrong side of satin. Wrap long edges of satin over poster board shape; glue in place. Repeat with short edges.

12. Matching bottom edges and beginning at center back, glue satin-covered poster board to outside of box overlapping ends.

13. Glue wrong side of remaining satin-covered box bottom to bottom of box.

14. Glue twisted satin cord around bottom of box.

15. Draw around box lid on batting two times. Cut one batting box lid on drawn line and one batting box lid ½" inside drawn line. Glue larger piece of batting to top of box lid. Center and glue smaller piece of batting on top of first piece of batting.

16. To cover box lid, cut a 9" x 27" bias strip of satin. Place a strip of double-stick tape around outside and inside edges of box lid. Beginning at center back and with right side facing out, position satin strip on tape on outside of box lid with satin strip extending 2" below lid. Trim short edge of satin strip 2" beyond center back. Turn unattached short edge 1" to wrong side. Use double-stick tape to hold folded edge of satin in place.

17. Fold satin strip to inside of box lid and press to tape on inside of box lid. Glue raw edges to inside of box lid. Glue satin-covered box top to inside of box lid.

18. Place a strip of double-stick tape on outside edge of box lid on top of satin. Beginning at center back, position ⅝"w ribbon around box lid on top of tape. Overlap ends 1"; trim excess ribbon. Turn short edge ½" to wrong side and secure with double-stick tape. Secure folded end of ribbon to box lid with double-stick tape.

19. Carefully apply Fray Check to remaining raw edge of satin strip; allow to dry.

20. To form pouf, hand baste satin strip approximately 2" from raw edge. Pull basting thread as tight as possible; secure and clip thread.

21. Tie double tassel satin cord in a bow around gathering line on satin.

22. To make nest for bird, wrap tulle around pouf; glue in place. Glue bird in nest.

23. Trim flowers and leaves from stem. Glue flowers and leaves around back and sides of nest.

BRIDESMAID'S PERFUME BOTTLE
Photo, page 37

SUPPLIES
Perfume bottle
¾ yd — ⅜"w satin ribbon
¼ yd — ⅛"w satin ribbon
Small ribbon rose
2 — 1⅜" lace heart motifs
1 pearl spray
Thick, clear-drying craft glue
Polyester fiberfill to stuff heart

INSTRUCTIONS
1. To make bow, measure to a starting point 2" from one end of ⅜"w ribbon and hold ribbon at this point between thumb and forefinger. For first loop, measure 3" from starting point and fold ribbon to form a loop by matching starting point and second point. Measure 3" from second point and form loop by matching second point and third point. Continue forming loops in this manner until you have four loops. Leave a 2" length of ribbon at the end of the fourth loop for streamer. Hand baste all loops and streamers together at the base of loops. Pull basting thread as tight as possible; secure and clip thread.

2. Cut a 9" length of ⅜"w ribbon; tie in a knot around bow. Tie bow to neck of bottle. Refer to Fig. 38 to fold and notch ribbon ends.

Fig. 38

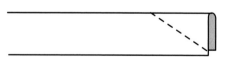

3. With wrong sides together, hand sew heart motifs together, leaving an opening on one side for stuffing. **Lightly** stuff heart with fiberfill. Whipstitch opening closed.

4. Fold ⅛"w ribbon in half; hand sew fold to center top of heart. Tie ribbon in a knot around neck of bottle. Trim ends of ⅛"w ribbon close to knot.

5. Glue pearl spray to bottle behind heart. Glue ribbon rose to heart.

8" x 10" HANGING PHOTO FRAME
Photo, page 40

SUPPLIES
8" x 10" covered frame kit
2 — 10" x 12" pieces of fleece
3 — 10" x 12" pieces of satin
3 — 10" x 12" pieces of fusible interfacing
3 yds — 6"w tulle
6" — 54"w dotted tulle
2¼ yds — 2"w satin ribbon
3⅛ yds — ¼"w satin ribbon
1¾ yds — 3mm strung iridescent beads
Thick, clear-drying craft glue

INSTRUCTIONS
1. Follow manufacturer's instructions to fuse interfacing to wrong side of satin pieces.

2. Follow manufacturer's instructions to cover frame pieces with satin using both pieces of fleece to pad frame. Do **not** assemble frame at this time.

3. For ruffle, cut two 54" x 3" lengths of dotted tulle. Machine stitch ¼"w ribbon to right side of each ruffle along one long edge; trim excess ribbon. Cut 6"w tulle into two 54" lengths. Matching long edges, fold each 6"w tulle length in half. Matching long raw edges, pin dotted tulle on top of folded tulle. Hand or machine baste ¼" from long raw edges. Pull basting thread until gathers measure 19½"; secure and clip thread. Fold each short end ½" to wrong side. Repeat with remaining lengths of tulle.

4. Glue each ruffle to back of frame front, beginning at bottom center.

5. Glue frame front to frame back, leaving top edge open to insert photo.

6. Glue beads to frame front.

7. To make bow, fold 2½" of one end of 2"w ribbon under to form first loop. Approximately 5¾" from folded end of first loop, fold ribbon under to form second loop. Approximately 5½" from folded end of second loop, fold ribbon under to form third loop. Approximately 5½" from folded end of third loop, fold ribbon under to form fourth loop; trim excess ribbon approximately 1" shorter than fourth loop. Hand baste through all layers at center of bow. Pull basting thread as tight as possible; secure and clip thread.

8. For streamers, match short ends and fold remaining 2"w ribbon in half; lightly crease center. Matching centers, tie ribbon in a knot around bow; bring streamers to back of bow.

9. For hanger, tie ends of remaining ¼"w ribbon in a knot. Hand sew to center back of bow.

10. Hand sew streamers to top center back of frame 4" from bow. Separate streamers slightly and hand sew to bottom center back of frame.

11. Refer to Fig. 39 to fold and notch ends of streamers at desired length.

Fig. 39

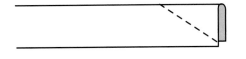

5" x 7" STANDING PHOTO FRAME

Photo, page 37

SUPPLIES

5" x 7" covered frame kit
2 — 6½" x 8½" pieces of fleece
3 — 6½" x 8½" pieces of satin
7½" x 5½" piece of satin to cover easel
3 — 6½" x 8½" pieces of fusible interfacing
⅝ yd — 2"w variegated wired ribbon
⅜ yd — 1"w wired ribbon
3" — ¼"w satin ribbon
2 — 1" velvet leaves
1¾ yds — 4mm strung pearls
Thick, clear-drying craft glue

INSTRUCTIONS

1. Follow manufacturer's instructions to fuse interfacing to wrong side of 6½" x 8½" satin pieces.

2. Follow manufacturer's instructions to cover frame pieces and easel with satin using both pieces of fleece to pad frame. Do **not** assemble frame at this time.

3. Hand baste along one long edge of 2"w ribbon. Pull basting thread until gathers measure 7"; secure and clip thread. Fold each short edge of ribbon at a 45° angle. Glue gathered edge of ribbon to wrong side of frame front.

4. Glue frame front to frame back, leaving top edge open to insert photo.

5. Follow manufacturer's instructions to apply easel and ¼"w ribbon to frame back.

6. Beginning and ending at top center of frame front, glue pearls around edge of frame front. Trim excess pearls.

7. Cut two 10" and two 8" lengths of pearls. Fold each length in half to form a loop; secure ends by wrapping with thread. Glue loops to top center of frame front.

8. For roses, cut three 3½" lengths of 1"w ribbon. Hand baste ¼" from one long edge of one ribbon length. Pull basting thread as tight as possible; secure and clip thread. Fold one short edge of length at a 45° angle *(Fig. 40)*; hand sew bottom edges together. For center of rose, keep edges even and turn point of ribbon to inside as shown in Fig. 41; hand sew edges together. Continue turning center of rose to inside and hand sewing edges together. At end of ribbon, fold remaining raw edge to back of rose at a 45° angle; hand sew in place. Secure and clip thread. Repeat with remaining lengths of ribbon. Glue ribbon roses to frame front on top of pearl loops.

Fig. 40

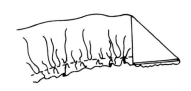

Fig. 41

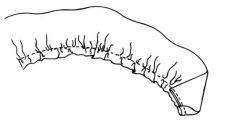

9. Glue leaves to frame front behind ribbon roses.

COVERED VIDEO TAPE BOX
Photo, page 39

SUPPLIES
5"w x 8"h x 1¼"d white video tape box
12¼" x 9" piece of moiré
2 — 11¼" x 8" pieces of fleece
1¼ yds twisted satin cord
1 yd — ⅞"w satin ribbon
Beaded lace motif
Thick, clear-drying craft glue
E-6000™ glue
1 sheet lightweight white poster board

INSTRUCTIONS
1. To find the natural bend of poster board, gently bend board vertically, then horizontally. The direction that poster board bends most easily is the natural bend. Place poster board on a flat work surface with natural bend running vertically.

2. Place opened tape box on poster board with spine of box running the same direction as natural bend of poster board. Draw around box, adding ½" to one short end to allow poster board to curve around spine of box; cut poster board along drawn lines.

3. Center both pieces of fleece on wrong side of moiré; place poster board on top of fleece.

4. Fold moiré over edges of poster board. Use craft glue to glue moiré in place. Do **not** glue corners at this time.

5. Wrap covered poster board around closed box to ease moiré and fleece around spine of box. Lightly crease poster board around spine of box.

6. Apply craft glue to both sides of corner fabric. Gently pull moiré over corners of poster board, creating small pleats; pin if necessary. Allow glue to dry; trim excess moiré from corners.

7. Use E-6000™ to glue covered poster board to box. Let glue dry in a well ventilated area 24 hours.

8. Beginning at center of long edge of box lid, use craft glue to glue cord around edges of box; trim excess cord.

9. Wrap ⅞"w ribbon around center of closed box; tie in a bow. Refer to Fig. 42 to fold and notch ribbon ends. Secure ribbon to box lid with small dot of craft glue.

Fig. 42

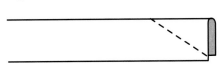

10. Use craft glue to glue beaded motif to box lid on top of ribbon.

8" x 10" STANDING PHOTO FRAME

SUPPLIES

8" x 10" covered frame kit
2 — 10" x 12" pieces of fleece
3 — 10" x 12" pieces of satin
9" x 8" piece of satin to cover easel
3 — 10" x 12" pieces of fusible interfacing
1½ yds — 2¼"w double-face satin ribbon
⅛ yd — ¼"w satin ribbon
½ yd — 4mm strung pearls
½ yd — 3mm strung iridescent beads
1 yd satin rattail cord
¼ yd beaded fringe
Thick, clear-drying craft glue

INSTRUCTIONS

1. Follow manufacturer's instructions to fuse interfacing to wrong side of 10" x 12" satin pieces.

2. Follow manufacturer's instructions to cover frame pieces and easel with satin using both pieces of fleece to pad frame. Do **not** assemble frame at this time.

3. Glue beaded fringe diagonally to frame sides *(Fig. 43)*.

Fig. 43

4. To make bow, fold 3½" of one end of 2¼"w ribbon under to form first loop. Approximately 5¼" from folded end of first loop, fold ribbon under to form second loop. Approximately 5¼" from folded end of second loop, fold ribbon under to form third loop. Approximately 6" from folded end of third loop, fold ribbon under to form fourth loop; trim excess ribbon approximately 1" shorter than third loop. Hand baste through all layers at center of bow. Pull basting thread as tight as possible; secure and clip thread.

5. For streamers, match short ends and fold remaining 2¼"w ribbon in half; lightly crease center. Matching centers, hand sew streamers to back of bow.

6. Cut beads and pearls in half. Holding one end of all lengths of beads and pearls together, tie lengths in an overhand knot. Place knot at center of bow; glue ends in place at back of bow.

7. Glue bow to top center of frame.

8. Drape ribbon streamers gracefully down frame sides. Glue streamers to frame front to hold drapes in place. Fold streamers diagonally where streamers meet beaded fringe *(Fig. 44)*; glue in place. Fold ends of ribbon to back of frame front; trim off excess ribbon. Glue ends to back of frame front.

Fig. 44

9. Glue frame front to frame back, leaving top edge open to insert photo.

10. Follow manufacturer's instructions to apply easel and ¼"w ribbon to frame back.

11. Beginning and ending at top center of frame front, glue satin cord around outer edge of frame front. Trim excess cord.

THE PERFECT
Wedding

Like beauty, the perfect wedding is in the eyes of the beholder. To have contemporary stylings or to hold to more traditional themes, ultimately a vision takes shape, and so begins the journey of transforming a little girl's fairy-tale wish into a woman's dream come true. A radiant bride, whether she's a satin sophisticate or an enchanted lady, graces everyone with a glimpse of essential loveliness.

BRIDE'S VEIL

SUPPLIES

Satin bridal cap
1½ yds — 54"w tulle
⅜ yd — 44/45"w satin
1 yd — ⅝"w braided trim
⅜ yd — ¼"w satin ribbon
2 yds — ⅜"w feather-edge satin ribbon
3½ yds — 3mm strung pearls
4 satin leaf clusters
3" clear plastic hair comb
Hot glue gun and glue sticks

INSTRUCTIONS

1. Beginning and ending at center back, glue braided trim to edge of cap.

2. Hand sew pearls to cap, attaching only at center front and center back.

3. To make veil, refer to Fig. 45 to fold tulle. To form pouf, hand or machine baste across width of veil 6" from folded edge. Run another basting thread ¼" from first basting thread. Pull both basting threads until gathers measure 8"; secure and clip threads.

Fig. 45

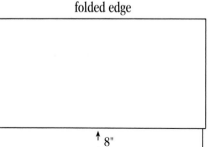

folded edge

8"

4. With pouf on top, match centers and glue or hand sew veil to back of cap.

5. For large roses, cut six 12" x 2½" lengths of satin. Fold one short end of one length ½" to wrong side; press. Matching wrong sides and long edges, fold length in half. Do **not** press. Hand or machine baste ¼" from long raw edge. Pull basting thread until gathers measure 10". Fold short unpressed edge of length at a 45° angle *(Fig. 46)*; hand sew bottom edges together. For center of rose, keep raw edges even and turn point of length to inside as shown in Fig. 47; hand sew raw edges together. Continue turning center of rose to inside and hand sewing raw edges together. At end of length, secure and clip thread. Repeat with remaining lengths of satin.

Fig. 46

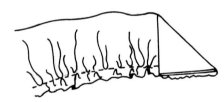

Fig. 47

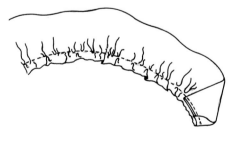

6. For small roses, cut five 6" x 1" lengths of satin. Follow Step 5 to make roses, pulling basting thread until gathers measure 5".

7. Refer to Fig. 48 to glue small roses, three large roses, and two leaf clusters in front of pouf at back of cap.

Fig. 48

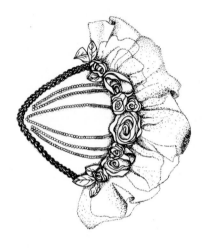

8. Cut one 19" length of feather-edge ribbon; match raw edges to form into loop. Hand sew raw edges of loop to center back of pouf along gathering line. Cut two 17" lengths of feather-edge ribbon; match raw edges to form into loops. Hand sew raw edges of loops to pouf along gathering line on each side of first loop. For streamers, cut two 8½" lengths of feather-edge ribbon; hand sew one end of each streamer to pouf on top of second loops.

9. Form remaining strung pearls into two 8" and two 6" loops. Glue or hand sew pearl loops on top of ribbon loops.

10. Refer to Fig. 49 to glue remaining large roses and leaf clusters on top of ribbon and pearl loops.

Fig. 49

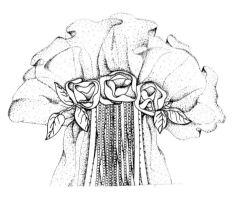

11. Working between teeth, use ¼"w ribbon to wrap top of comb. Use glue to secure ends of ribbon to comb.

12. Matching centers, hand sew comb to under side of back of cap.

BRIDESMAID'S HAT

SUPPLIES
Satin bridal cap
⅝ yd — 44/45"w satin
5" x 72" piece of net
¾ yd — ½"w lace trim
⅜ yd — ¼"w satin ribbon
¾ yd — lace seam binding
6 pearl loops
3" clear plastic hair comb
Hot glue gun and glue sticks
Tracing paper
Thumbtack
16" piece of string

INSTRUCTIONS

1. For pattern to cover cap, cut a 15" square of tracing paper. To draw cutting line, tie one end of string to pencil near tip. Insert thumbtack in string 13½" from pencil. Insert thumbtack through corner of paper; draw one-fourth of a circle *(Fig. 50)*. Cut out pattern. Pin pattern to satin; cut out satin piece.

Fig. 50

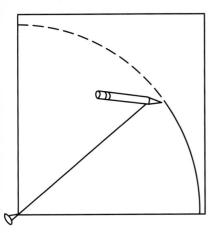

2. With rounded edge of satin to back of cap and satin extending ½" beyond cap edges, wrap satin over cap. Smoothly fold satin to inside of cap at front and sides; glue in place, stopping 3" from center back on both sides. Fold pleats in satin as shown in Fig. 51; adjust to fit back of cap. Pin pleats in place. Trim excess satin so that satin extends ½" beyond cap edges. Fold pleated satin to inside of cap at back and glue in place; remove pins.

Fig. 51

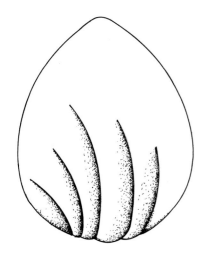

3. Covering raw edge of satin, glue lace seam binding to inside of cap. Trim excess seam binding.

4. Beginning at center back, glue lace trim to outside edge of cap. Trim excess lace.

5. To make pouf, match short edges and fold piece of net in half. Hand or machine baste through both layers of net ½" and ¼" from one long edge. Pull both basting threads until gathers measure 3"; secure and clip threads. Glue pouf above lace trim at back of cap along gathering lines.

6. For bow, cut a 3½" x 27" piece of satin. Fold each short end ¼" to wrong side; press. To form each point, fold ends as shown in Fig. 52. Fold each long edge 1" to wrong side; press.

Fig. 52

7. Matching points and wrong sides, fold piece in half. Lightly crease center. Pin and stitch across satin 3½" from points (*Fig. 53*). Pin and stitch across satin 9" from points (*Fig. 54*).

Fig. 53

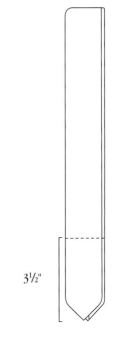

3½"

Fig. 54

9"

8. Lay satin piece on work surface with points facing out. Match seams to form first loops; hold in place. Match center to seams for second loops; pin in place. Stitch center of bow through all thicknesses as shown in Fig. 55; remove pins.

Fig. 55

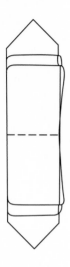

9. For center piece of bow, cut a 1½" x 2½" piece of satin. Fold each short edge ¼" to wrong side; press. Fold each long edge ½" to wrong side; press. Wrap center piece around bow, placing wrong side over stitching line. Hand sew short ends together at back of bow.

10. Glue bow to back of cap on top of net. Glue pearl loops between layers of net as desired.

11. Working between teeth, use ribbon to wrap top of comb. Use glue to secure ends of ribbon to comb.

12. Matching centers, hand sew comb to inside back of cap.

BRIDE'S BOUQUET

SUPPLIES
1⅜" x 3½" bouquet holder
9" dia. lace bouquet collar
⅜ yd — 44/45"w white satin
½ yd — 44/45"w white printed satin for roses
1 yd — 6"w white tulle
⅞ yd — 6"w colored tulle
⅞ yd — 4"w colored satin florist ribbon
1⅜ yds — 2"w white double-face satin ribbon
2⅜ yds — ¼"w colored double-face satin ribbon
6" — ⅛"w colored satin ribbon
1 colored silk blossom spray
6 small leaves
5 large leaves
6 colored pearl loops
Hot glue gun and glue sticks (optional)
Thick, clear-drying craft glue
Craft scissors or wire cutters
Floral picks
Floral pins
Floral tape

Please familiarize yourself with basic techniques found in General Instructions, pg. 108, before beginning project. The measurements on the Placement Diagram indicate the length of the stem from the base of the flower, lowest leaf, or base of pearl loop.

INSTRUCTIONS
1. Refer to Placement Diagram, pg. 52, for measurements and follow Preparing Flowers and Greenery, pg. 108, to separate, trim, and wrap stems of all flowers, greenery, and pearl loops.

2. Insert handle of bouquet holder through center of bouquet collar; glue in place.

3. Cut one 20" x 10" length of satin. Fold short edges ½" to wrong side; press. Matching right sides and long edges, fold length in half; pin in place. Using a ½" seam allowance, machine stitch long edges together; remove pins. Turn right side out; press seamed edge only.

4. Machine baste ¼" from seamed edge. Pull basting thread until gathers measure 8"; secure and clip thread. Glue satin to bouquet collar as shown in Fig. 56. Lightly stuff satin with white tulle.

Fig. 56

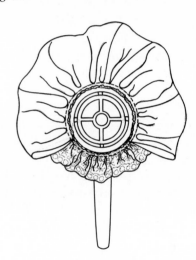

5. To make double bow, fold 4"w ribbon into thirds (Fig. 57). Repeat with colored tulle.

Fig. 57

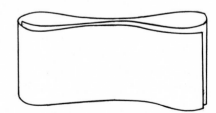

6. Place tulle bow on top of satin bow. Tie ⅛"w ribbon in a knot around center of bows, gathering both bows; trim ⅛"w ribbon ends close to knot. Glue double bow to center front of bouquet holder.

7. For large roses, cut ten 2½" x 12" lengths of printed satin. Fold short ends of one length ½" to wrong side; press. Matching wrong sides and long edges, fold length in half. Do **not** press. Hand or machine baste ¼" from long edges. Pull basting thread as tight as possible;

secure and clip thread. Begin with one short end of length and roll ¼" to inside, keeping raw edges even. Hand sew raw edges together. Continue rolling length to inside and hand sewing edges together. At end of length, secure and clip thread. Repeat with remaining lengths of satin.

8. For small roses, cut six 2" x 11" lengths of printed satin. Follow Step 7 to make roses.

9. Refer to Assembling Bouquets, pg. 109, to insert floral pin in each rose. Insert floral-pinned roses into center and outer rings of bouquet holder.

10. Refer to Placement Diagram to insert blossoms, pearl loops, and leaves into bouquet holder.

11. To make white bow, measure to a starting point 13½" from one end of 2"w ribbon and hold ribbon at this point between thumb and forefinger. For first loop, measure 10" from starting point and fold ribbon to form a loop by matching starting point and second point. Measure 10" from second point and form loop by matching second point and third point. Leave a 13½" length of ribbon at the end of the second loop for streamer. Hand baste all loops and streamers together at the base of loops. Pull basting thread as tight as possible; secure and clip thread. Glue white bow on top of double bow.

PLACEMENT DIAGRAM

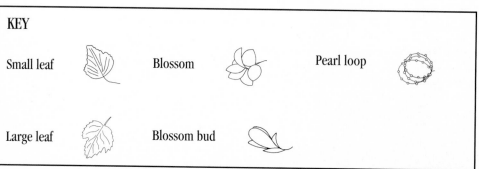

KEY

Small leaf   Blossom   Pearl loop

Large leaf   Blossom bud

52

12. To make colored bow, measure to a starting point 7" from one end of ¼"w ribbon and hold ribbon at this point between thumb and forefinger. For first loop, measure 18" from starting point and fold ribbon to form a loop by matching starting point and second point. Measure 18" from second point and form loop by matching second point and third point. Measure 14" from third point and form loop by matching third point and fourth point. Measure 12" from fourth point and form loop by matching fourth point and fifth point. Leave an 11" length of ribbon at the end of the fourth loop for streamer. Hand baste all loops and streamers together at the base of loops. Pull basting thread as tight as possible; secure and clip thread. Glue colored bow to center of white bow.

BRIDESMAID'S BOUQUET

SUPPLIES
9" x 20" piece of satin
¼ yd — 1½"w satin ribbon to cover stems
2½ yds — 1"w brocade ribbon
3 small silk hydrangea stems
Hot glue gun and glue sticks (optional)
Thick, clear-drying craft glue
Craft scissors or wire cutters
Floral tape

Please familiarize yourself with basic techniques found in General Instructions, pg. 108, before beginning project. The measurements on the Placement Diagram indicate the length of the stem from the base of the flower or lowest leaf.

INSTRUCTIONS

1. Trim hydrangea stems to 5". Follow Preparing Flowers and Greenery, pg. 108, to join stems together with floral tape beginning 1½" below lowest leaf. Wrap stems with 1½"w ribbon to cover tape. Trim excess ribbon; glue in place.

2. Fold short edges of satin ½" to wrong side; press. Matching right sides and long edges, fold satin in half. Pin and stitch long edges together using ¼" seam allowance; remove pins. Turn right side out; press seamed edge only. Machine baste ½" from seamed edge. Pull basting thread until gathers measure 6"; secure and clip thread. Glue gathering line of satin to back of flower stems.

3. To make ribbon loops, measure to a starting point 9" from one end of 1"w ribbon and hold ribbon at this point between thumb and forefinger. For first loop, measure 24" from starting point and fold ribbon to form a loop by matching starting point and second point. Measure 23" from second point and form loop by matching second point and third point. Measure 12" from third point and form loop by matching third point and fourth point. Measure 10" from fourth point and form loop by matching fourth point and fifth point. Leave a 9" length of ribbon at the end of the fourth loop for streamer. Hand baste all loops and streamers together at base of loops. Pull basting thread as tight as possible; secure and clip thread.

4. Glue ribbon loops to front of stems below hydrangea leaves.

BRIDESMAID'S BAG

SUPPLIES

⅝ yd — 44/45"w colored satin
2" x 12" piece of white lightweight printed satin
2 — 9" x 7" pieces of polyester batting
8½" x 6½" piece of paper-backed fusible web
3⅜ yds — 1"w colored wired ribbon
1¼ yds — 6mm strung pearls
Large covered snap
Fray Check™
Tracing paper

INSTRUCTIONS

(Note: For all machine stitching, use ½" seam allowance. Backstitch at the beginning and end of each seam.)

1. Cut six 9" and eight 7" lengths of ribbon. Apply Fray Check to all ribbon ends; allow to dry. Working on ironing board and with 9" lengths running horizontally and 7" lengths running vertically, weave ribbons. As each ribbon is woven, pin in place on ironing board.

2. Follow manufacturer's instructions to fuse web to center of woven ribbons. Remove paper backing. Follow manufacturer's instructions to fuse one piece of batting to web side of woven ribbons.

3. Cut three 9" x 7" pieces of colored satin. Hand baste remaining piece of batting to wrong side of one 9" x 7" piece of colored satin.

4. For lining, match right sides and raw edges of remaining 9" x 7" pieces of colored satin; pin and stitch two short edges and one long edge. Press raw edge ½" to wrong side. Set lining aside.

5. For ruffle, fold tracing paper in half and place folded edge along heavy solid line on pattern (shown in grey on page 110). Use pencil to trace pattern on tracing paper, matching dashed lines to extend pattern; cut out traced pattern. Unfold pattern and lay it flat. Cut out two colored satin ruffles.

6. Fold short ends of one ruffle ½" to wrong side; press. Matching wrong sides and long edges, fold ruffle in half. Do **not** press. Machine baste through both layers ¼" from long edges. Run another basting thread ⅛" from first basting thread. Pull both basting threads until gathers measure 7½"; secure and clip threads. Repeat with remaining ruffle.

7. Center one ruffle on right side of woven ribbons, matching raw edges of ruffle to one long edge of woven ribbons; pin and stitch. Center remaining ruffle on right side of satin piece with batting, matching raw edges of ruffle to one long edge of satin piece; pin and stitch. Press seam allowances away from ruffles.

8. Matching right sides and raw edges, pin and stitch woven ribbon piece and satin piece together leaving edges with ruffles unstitched. Trim seam allowances to ¼"; clip corners. Turn bag right side out.

9. Insert lining into bag, matching wrong side of lining to wrong side of bag. Hand sew folded edge of lining to stitching line of ruffle. Hand sew snap to lining of bag.

10. For strap, hand sew one end of pearls to one side seam. To form loop, measure 4" from sewn end of pearls. Hand sew this point to side seam. Repeat to attach remaining end of pearls and to make loop on remaining side seam.

11. For large rose, fold one short end of lightweight printed satin ½" to wrong side; press. Matching wrong sides and long edges, fold length in half. Do **not** press. Hand or machine baste ¼" from long raw edges. Pull basting thread as tight as possible; secure and clip thread. Fold short unpressed edges of length at a 45° angle *(Fig. 58)*; hand sew bottom edges together. For center of rose, keep raw edges even and turn point of length to inside as shown in Fig. 59; hand sew raw edges together. Continue turning center of rose to inside and hand sewing raw edges together. At end of length, secure and clip thread.

Fig. 58

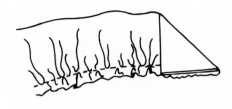

Fig. 59

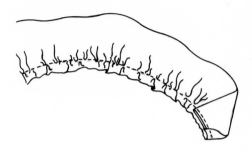

12. For small rose, cut a 1" x 5" length of colored satin. Follow Step 11 to make rose.

13. Hand sew roses to bag.

GARTER
Photo, page 55

SUPPLIES
2½" x 8" piece of colored satin
3 yds — 2½"w flat white lace (with one straight edge)
1 yd — ⅞"w white satin ribbon
½ yd — ⅝"w white satin ribbon
½ yd — ⅜"w colored satin ribbon
½ yd — ⅜"w elastic
⅜ yd — 4mm colored strung pearls
8mm pearl
Hot glue gun and glue sticks

INSTRUCTIONS
1. Cut lace into three 36" lengths. With right sides up, refer to Fig. 60 to place one length of lace over second length of lace. Pin and stitch through both layers 1" from straight edge of top layer of lace. This will be the right side of the garter.

Fig. 60

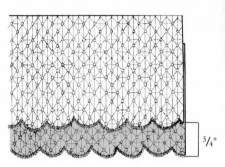

¾"

2. With right sides up, refer to Fig. 61 to place sewn lengths of lace over remaining length of lace. Pin and stitch through all layers 1" from top scalloped edge of lace.

Fig. 61

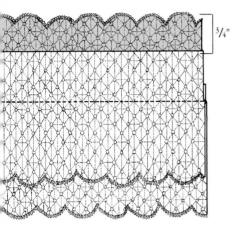

3. For casing, match one long edge of ⅞"w ribbon to top straight edge of lace. Stitch ribbon to lace along both long edges through all layers. On **wrong side**, trim straight edge of lace ¼" below lowest stitching line of casing.

4. Insert elastic into casing. Adjust elastic to fit bride's leg; pin ends of elastic in place. Matching right sides and short edges of lace, pin and stitch short edges together using ¼" seam allowance. Stitch again ⅛" from raw edges; trim seam allowances close to second line of stitching.

5. Holding ⅜"w ribbon and ⅝"w ribbon together, tie ribbon lengths in a bow. Refer to Fig. 62 to fold and notch ribbon ends. Hand sew bow to front of garter over casing.

Fig. 62

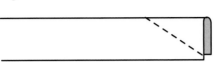

6. For loops, cut pearls in half. Fold each length in half to form a loop; secure ends by wrapping with thread. Hand sew wrapped end of each loop to center of bow.

7. For rose, use colored satin and follow Step 11 of Enchanted Moment Bridesmaid's Bag, pg. 56. Glue 8mm pearl in center of rose. Hand sew rose to center of bow on top of pearl loops.

BRIDE'S SHOES
Photo, page 55

SUPPLIES
1 pair satin shoes
1 pair shoe clips
⅔ yd — 2"w flat white lace (with one straight edge)
2 — 2" x 12" pieces of colored satin
⅝ yd — ⅜"w colored satin ribbon

INSTRUCTIONS
1. Cut lace in half. Fold each raw edge to wrong side at a 45° angle. Hand baste ¼" from long straight edge of one length of lace. Pull basting thread as tight as possible; secure and clip thread. Hand sew gathered edge of lace to shoe clip. Repeat with remaining length of lace and shoe clip.

2. For each rose, use one satin piece and follow Step 11 of Enchanted Moment Bridesmaid's Bag, pg. 56. Hand sew one rose to lace on each shoe clip.

3. Cut ribbon in half. Tie each ribbon length in a bow. Hand sew one bow to lace below each satin rose. Clip to toes of shoes. Refer to Fig. 63 to fold and notch ribbon ends.

Fig. 63

BRIDE'S HAT

SUPPLIES

Satin bridal hat
1 yd — 44/45"w lightweight printed satin for brim
⅝ yd — 44/45"w satin for back decoration and rose
1 yd — ¼"w satin ribbon
¾ yd lace seam binding
2 yds — 6mm strung pearls
3" clear plastic hair comb
Hot glue gun and glue sticks

INSTRUCTIONS

1. To cover brim of hat, cut a bias strip of lightweight printed satin twice the measurement of outer edge of hat brim and twice the width of the brim plus 1" (pieced if necessary). Fold short ends of bias strip ½" to wrong side; press. Hand or machine baste ½" and ¼" from both long edges.

2. Pull basting threads on one long edge and place bias strip over brim with ½" gathering line placed along base of crown; overlap ends 1". Adjust gathers to fit base of crown and glue gathers in place. Trim excess fabric above gathering stitches.

3. Pull remaining basting threads and place ½" gathering line along base of crown inside hat. Adjust gathers to fit base of crown and glue gathers in place. Trim excess fabric above gathering stitches.

4. Covering raw edge, glue lace seam binding over gathered edge of bias strip on inside of hat.

5. Beginning at center back on outside of hat, glue one row of pearls to bias strip on top of gathering line. Cut off excess pearls. Repeat with remaining pearls to add two more rows.

6. To decorate back of hat, cut two 22" x 11" lengths of satin. Fold short ends 1" to wrong side; press. Matching wrong sides and long edges, fold each length in half. Do **not** press. Hand or machine baste ¼" and ⅛" from raw edges. Pull both basting threads until gathers measure 4"; secure and clip threads. Refer to Fig. 64 and fold each strip into a "U" shape.

Fig. 64

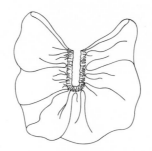

7. Glue gathered edges of strips to center back of hat as shown in Fig. 65.

Fig. 65

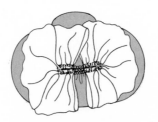

8. Crush and drape strips around crown and brim. Use glue to hold draped folds in place.

9. For rose, cut one 25" x 6" length of satin. Fold one short end ½" to wrong side; press. Matching wrong sides and long edges, fold length in half. Do **not** press. Hand or machine baste ¼" from long raw edge. Pull basting thread until gathers measure 21". Fold short unpressed edge of length at a 45° angle *(Fig. 66);* hand sew bottom edges together. For center of rose, keep raw edges even and turn point of length to inside as shown in Fig. 67. Hand sew raw edges together. Continue turning center of rose to inside and hand sewing raw edges together. At end of length, secure and clip thread. Glue rose to center back of hat on top of draped folds.

Fig. 66

Fig. 67

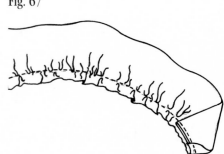

10. Working between teeth, use ¼"w ribbon to wrap top of comb. Use glue to secure ends of ribbon to comb.

11. Matching centers, hand sew comb to back of hat along inside crown line.

BRIDESMAID'S HAT
Photo, page 60

SUPPLIES

Mesh bridal hat
1 yd — 44/45"w satin
1 yd — 6"w tulle
5½ yds — ¼"w satin ribbon
¾ yd — ⅝"w satin ribbon
4½ yds — 3mm strung pearls
3" clear plastic hair comb
Hot glue gun and glue sticks

INSTRUCTIONS

1. Weave ¼"w ribbon through crown of hat. Cut and glue ends of each ribbon length to wrong side of brim at front and back of hat.

2. To cover brim of hat, cut a bias strip of satin twice the measurement of outer edge of hat brim and twice the width of the brim plus 1" (pieced if necessary). Fold short ends of bias strip ½" to wrong side; press. Hand or machine baste ½" and ¼" from both long edges.

3. Pull basting threads on one long edge and place bias strip over brim with ½" gathering line placed along base of crown; overlap ends 1". Adjust gathers to fit base of crown and glue gathers in place. Trim excess fabric above gathering stitches.

4. Pull remaining basting threads and place ½" gathering line along base of crown inside hat. Adjust gathers to fit base of crown and glue gathers in place. Trim excess fabric above gathering stitches.

5. Covering raw edge, glue ⅝"w ribbon over gathered edge of bias strip on inside of hat. Trim excess ribbon.

6. Cut five 27" lengths of pearls. Secure one end of all lengths together by wrapping with thread. Glue wrapped end of pearl lengths to center back of hat at base of crown. Holding lengths together, gently twist pearls. Covering raw edge of satin, glue twisted pearls to crown at 1" intervals, ending at center back. Trim excess pearls.

7. Glue remaining pearl length to crown just above twisted pearls. Trim excess pearls.

8. Cut two 36" lengths of ¼"w ribbon. Machine stitch one ribbon length to each long edge of tulle. Hand or machine baste along length of tulle 2½" from one long edge. Run another basting thread ¼" from first basting thread. Pull basting threads until gathers measure 3½"; secure and clip threads.

9. Placing 2½" portion of tulle next to brim of hat and 3½" portion of tulle next to crown of hat, match centers and glue tulle to back of hat on top of pearls along gathering lines. Glue raw edges of tulle to pearls.

10. For roses, cut four 2½" x 8" lengths of satin. Fold one short end of one length ½" to wrong side; press. Matching wrong sides and long edges, fold length in half. Do **not** press. Hand or machine baste ¼" from long raw edges. Pull basting thread until gathers measure 6½". Fold short unpressed edges of length at a 45° angle *(Fig. 68);* hand sew bottom edges together. For center of rose, keep raw edges even and turn point of length to inside as shown in Fig. 69; hand sew raw edges together. Continue turning center of rose to inside and hand sewing raw edges together. At end of length, secure and clip thread. Repeat with remaining lengths of satin.

Fig. 68

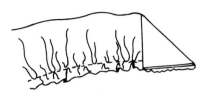

Fig. 69

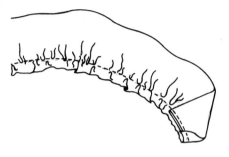

11. Refer to Fig. 70 and glue roses to back of hat on gathering line of tulle.

Fig. 70

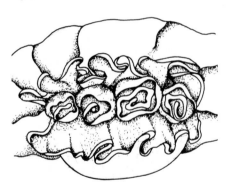

12. Working between teeth, use remaining ¼"w ribbon to wrap top of comb. Use glue to secure ends of ribbon to comb.

13. Matching centers, hand sew comb to back of hat along inside crown line.

BRIDE'S BOUQUET
Photo, page 62

SUPPLIES

1 yd — 44/45"w satin
1⅓ yds — ¼"w satin ribbon
1¾ yds — 3"w iridescent honeycomb ribbon
2 silk gladiolus stems
2 silk rosebud stems (5 buds each)
Floral tape

Please familiarize yourself with basic techniques found in General Instructions, pg. 108, before beginning project. The measurements on the Placement Diagram indicate the length of the stem from the base of the flower or lowest leaf.

INSTRUCTIONS

1. Follow Preparing Flowers and Greenery, pg. 108, to wrap stems of all flowers with floral tape. Holding all flowers together, arrange as desired. Begin just below lowest blossom and tape all stems together for 6".

2. For satin bow, cut one 24" x 20½" piece of satin. Matching right sides and long raw edges, fold piece in half. Using a ½" seam allowance, pin and stitch long edges together; remove pins. Turn right side out; press. Matching short ends, fold satin piece in half; lightly crease center. Unfold satin piece. Place satin piece on work surface. Fold each short end to center, overlapping center crease by ½"; pin in place. Machine baste across center of satin piece, stitching through all layers. Remove pins. Pull basting thread as tight as possible to gather satin piece into bow; secure and clip thread.

3. For bow knot, cut a 2½" x 4½" piece of satin. Turn all raw edges ½" to wrong side; press. Wrap knot around center of bow over basting thread. Overlap ends ½"; hand sew in place.

4. For streamer, cut one 12" x 40" piece of satin. Matching right sides and long edges, fold piece in half. Using a ½" seam allowance, pin and stitch long edges together leaving a 4" opening at center for turning; remove pins.

5. Measure in ½" on seam line and **lightly** mark with pencil. Measure in 6" on fold and **lightly** mark with pencil. Use ruler and **lightly** draw a line on satin connecting the pencil markings *(Fig. 71)*. Repeat with remaining end. Stitch along drawn lines. Trim corners. Turn right side out; press. Slipstitch opening closed. Matching diagonal ends, fold streamer in half; lightly crease center. Machine baste along center crease. Pull basting thread as tight as possible; secure and clip thread.

Fig. 71

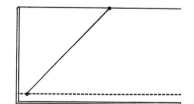

6. Cut a 24" length of ¼"w ribbon. Matching raw edges, fold ribbon in half; lightly crease center. Matching centers, place ribbon on streamer along gathering line as shown in Fig. 72; pin in place. Stitch ribbon to streamer along gathering line; remove pins.

Fig. 72

7. Matching centers, hand sew bow to streamer.

8. To add streamer to bouquet, thread ¼"w ribbon on streamer through flower stems just above point where stems are taped together. Tie ribbon in a knot close to stems.

9. To make honeycomb bow, measure to a starting point 21" from one end of ribbon and hold ribbon at this point between thumb and forefinger. For first loop, measure 9½" from starting point and fold ribbon to form a loop by matching starting point and second point. Measure 9½" from second point and form loop by matching second point and third point. Leave a 21" length of ribbon at the end of the second loop for streamer. Tie remaining ¼"w ribbon in a knot around base of loops and streamers. Tie ribbon on honeycomb bow in a knot around flower stems on top of satin bow.

BRIDESMAID'S BOUQUET

SUPPLIES
1½ yds — 6"w colored tulle
3⅞ yds — 2¼"w white double-face satin ribbon
2 white silk gladiolus stems
3 — 17" grass stems
Hot glue gun and glue sticks
Craft scissors or wire cutters
Floral tape
Floral wire

Please familiarize yourself with basic techniques found in General Instructions, pg. 108, before beginning project. The measurements on the Placement Diagram indicate the length of the stem from the base of the flower or lowest leaf.

INSTRUCTIONS
1. Follow Preparing Flowers and Greenery, pg. 108, to wrap stems of all flowers with floral tape. Holding all flowers and leaves together, arrange as desired. Beginning 5" below lowest blossom, join all stems together with floral tape for 4".

2. For bow, measure to a starting point 18" from one end of 2¼"w ribbon and hold ribbon at this point between thumb and forefinger. For first loop, measure 12" from starting point and fold ribbon to form a loop by matching starting point and second point. Measure 12" from second point and form loop by matching second point and third point. Continue forming loops in this manner until you have eight loops. For small loop, measure 5" from last point and fold loop as above. Leave a 15" length of ribbon at the end of the small loop for streamer. Secure center of all loops with floral wire. Pull small loop to front of bow to cover floral wire; glue in place.

3. To make tulle loops, cut five 10" lengths of tulle. Matching short edges, fold one length in half. Baste ¼" from raw edges. Gather ends to measure 1" *(Fig. 73);* secure and clip thread. Repeat with remaining lengths of tulle. Glue tulle loops between bow loops.

Fig. 73

4. Wrap wire from bow around stems of flowers 5" below lowest blossom; secure and clip wire. Wrap remaining 2¼"w ribbon around flower stems to cover wire; glue in place. Trim excess ribbon.

GARTER
Photo, page 64

SUPPLIES
2 — 2½" squares of satin for leaves
1 yd — 6"w tulle
1 yd — ⅝"w satin ribbon
1 yd — ¼"w satin ribbon
½ yd — ⅜"w elastic
3 small silk flowers
4 tiny silk flowers
1 pkg 3mm pearls
Hot glue gun and glue sticks
Jewel glue
Fray Check™

INSTRUCTIONS
1. Stitch ¼"w ribbon to one long edge of tulle.

2. To form casing, fold remaining long edge of tulle 1½" to right side; press. Covering raw edge of tulle, place ⅝"w ribbon on tulle with top edge of ribbon 1" from folded edge of tulle. Stitch ribbon to tulle along both long edges.

3. Use jewel glue to attach pearls to right side of tulle, leaving ½" unbeaded along short edges.

4. Insert elastic into casing. Adjust elastic to fit bride's leg; pin ends of elastic in place. Matching right sides and short edges of tulle, pin and stitch short edges together using ¼" seam allowance. Stitch again ⅛" from raw edges; trim seam allowances close to second line of stitching.

5. For satin leaves, match wrong sides and fold one satin square in half to form a triangle. Bring folded outer points to center point as shown in Fig. 74, forming a diamond; pin points in place. Hand baste across points as shown in Fig. 75. Pull basting thread until gathers measure ¾"; secure and clip thread. Trim raw edges ¼" below gathers. Repeat with remaining satin square. Apply Fray Check to cut edges; allow to dry.

Fig. 74

Fig. 75

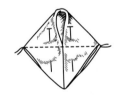

6. Hand sew satin leaves to casing at front of garter. Hot glue flowers on top of satin leaves.

RICE CRACKER
Photo, page 64

SUPPLIES
(**Note**: Supplies are for making one rice cracker.)
- 4" x 6" piece of satin
- ¾ yd — 4"w pregathered nylon ruffle
- 2" x 4¾" piece of fusible interfacing
- ¼ yd — ⅜"w satin ribbon
- 20" — ¼"w satin ribbon
- 3 small silk flowers
- Hot glue gun and glue sticks
- Thick, clear-drying craft glue
- 2" x 1¼" dia. cardboard tube (We used a gift wrap tube.)
- 2 — 2" squares of white poster board
- ¼" hole punch
- Rice or birdseed

INSTRUCTIONS
1. Follow manufacturer's instructions to fuse interfacing to center of wrong side of satin piece.

2. Matching right sides and short edges of satin, pin and stitch short edges together using ½" seam allowance. Press seam allowances open. Turn tube right side out. Insert cardboard tube into satin tube.

3. Fold raw edges of satin tube into cardboard tube; use craft glue to secure in place.

4. Cut two 5" lengths of ¼"w ribbon. Glue one ribbon length around each end of satin tube.

5. Tie ⅜"w ribbon in a bow. Hot glue bow and silk flowers to center of tube. Trim ribbon ends as desired.

6. Cut nylon ruffle in half. Hand or machine baste ½" from gathered edge of one length. Pull basting thread as tight as possible; secure and clip thread.

7. For ribbon pull, match raw edges and fold remaining ¼"w ribbon in half. Measure 4" from fold. Hand sew this point to one end of gathered edge of remaining ruffle. Loop of ribbon pull should extend toward finished edge of ruffle. Hand or machine baste ½" from gathered edge. Pull basting thread as tight as possible; secure and clip thread. Trim ribbon ends as desired.

8. Cut two poster board circles the diameter of inside of tube. Mark center of one circle with pencil. Make ¼" hole at pencil mark with hole punch. Cut from outer edge of circle to punched hole. Repeat with remaining circle.

9. Slip gathered edge of one nylon ruffle into center of one poster board circle through slit on outer edge. Repeat with remaining ruffle and circle. Insert one circle into one end of tube. Fill tube with rice, leaving enough space to insert remaining circle. Insert remaining circle into open end of tube.

BRIDESMAID'S SHOES
Photo, page 64

SUPPLIES
- 1 pair dyed satin shoes
- 2 — 18" x 2" pieces of tulle
- 1 yd — ¼"w satin ribbon
- 6 small silk flowers
- 3 yds — 4mm strung pearls
- Hot glue gun and glue sticks
- Jewel glue

INSTRUCTIONS
1. Beginning and ending at center front, use jewel glue to attach pearls to top edge of one shoe; trim excess pearls. Beginning and ending at center front, glue second string of pearls below first string, placing pearls right below first string at top of shoe and 1" below first string at back of shoe. Trim excess pearls. Repeat with remaining shoe.

2. Cut ribbon in half. Stitch one length of ribbon to one long edge of each length of tulle.

3. Matching short edges, fold one length of tulle in half; lightly crease center. Unfold tulle. With right side down, place tulle on work surface. Fold each short edge to center, overlapping center crease by ¼"; pin in place. Hand or machine baste ¼" from long, raw edge of tulle. Pull basting thread as tight as possible; secure and clip thread. Repeat with remaining length of tulle.

4. Hot glue one tulle pouf and three small flowers to each shoe.

BRIDE'S SHOES

SUPPLIES
- 1 pair satin shoes
- 1 pair lace motifs
- 3mm strung pearls
- Pearls and/or pearl beads (We used 5mm pearls and 7mm oblong pearl beads.)
- Jewel glue

INSTRUCTIONS
1. Glue motifs to shoes. Glue strung pearls, pearls, and pearl beads to shoes as desired.

BRIDE'S VEIL

SUPPLIES

1 yd — 54"w tulle
1⅛ yds — ¼"w satin ribbon
2 — 6" floral sprays with pearls
White floral tape
3" clear plastic hair comb
Hot glue gun and glue sticks

INSTRUCTIONS

1. To form floral crown, place floral sprays together end to end, overlapping stems 1" *(Fig. 76)*. Wrap overlapped stems with floral tape.

Fig. 76

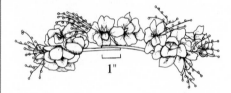

2. Cut a 27" length of ribbon. Glue one end of ribbon to one end of stems. With edges of ribbon touching, but not overlapping, cover stems by wrapping and gluing ribbon around stems. Trim excess ribbon; glue end of ribbon to stems.

3. To make veil, hand or machine baste across width of tulle 18" from one long edge. Run another basting thread ¼" from first basting thread. Pull both basting threads until gathers measure 4"; secure and clip threads. Matching centers, hand sew veil to stems of floral crown along gathering line.

4. Working between teeth, use remaining ribbon to wrap top of comb. Use glue to secure ends of ribbon to comb.

5. Matching centers, hand sew comb to veil and stems of floral crown.

6. Bend floral crown into arch to fit bride's head.

BRIDESMAID'S HAIR PIECE

SUPPLIES

1 silk snapdragon stem
⅝ yd — 1½"w colored wired ribbon
1⅓ yds — 1"w variegated wired ribbon
1 yd — 1"w white wired ribbon
⅜ yd — ¼"w colored satin ribbon
1 pkg pearl stamens
15mm plastic barrette
3" clear plastic hair comb
Hot glue gun and glue sticks
Wire cutters

INSTRUCTIONS

1. Cut a 5" length of 1½"w wired ribbon. Cover plastic barrette with ribbon; glue ends to back.

2. Use wire cutters to trim snapdragon stem to approximately 12". Hand sew large end to ribbon on barrette top as shown in Fig. 77.

Fig. 77

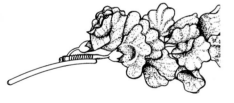

3. Working between teeth, use ¼"w ribbon to wrap top of comb. Use glue to secure ends of ribbon to comb. Matching centers, glue comb to back of barrette.

4. For buds, cut four 2½" lengths of 1"w variegated wired ribbon. Fold one short edge of length at a 45° angle (Fig. 78); hand sew bottom edges together. For center of bud, keep edges even and turn point of ribbon to inside as shown in Fig. 79; hand sew edges together. Continue turning center of bud to inside and hand sewing edges together. At end of ribbon, secure and clip thread. Repeat with remaining lengths of ribbon.

Fig. 78

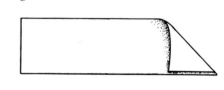

Fig. 79

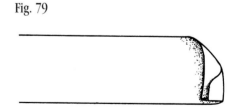

5. For rosettes, cut six 6" lengths of 1"w variegated wired ribbon. Hand baste ¼" from one long edge of one ribbon length. Pull basting thread until gathers measure 4½". Fold one short edge of length at a 45° angle *(Fig. 80)*; hand sew bottom edges together. For center of rosette, keep edges even and turn point of ribbon to inside as shown in Fig. 81; hand sew edges together. Continue turning center of rosette to inside and hand sewing edges together. At end of ribbon, secure and clip thread. Repeat with remaining lengths of ribbon. Glue several stamens into center of each rosette.

Fig. 80

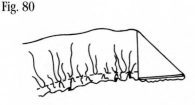

Fig. 81

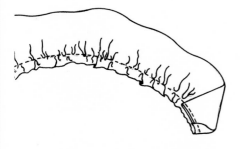

6. For large roses, cut two 7" lengths of 1½"w wired ribbon. Baste ¼" from one long edge of one ribbon length. Pull basting thread as tight as possible; secure and clip thread. Fold each end of ribbon to outside of rose at a 45° angle. Repeat with remaining length of ribbon.

7. Insert one rosette into each large rose as shown in Fig. 82; hand sew bottom edges together.

Fig. 82

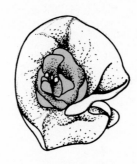

8. Refer to Fig. 83 and glue large roses, buds, and remaining rosettes into snapdragon stem.

Fig. 83

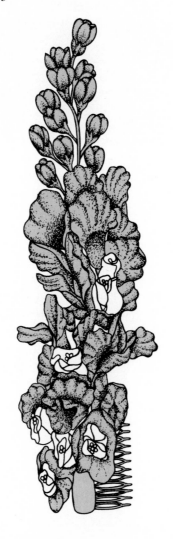

9. For bow, cut a 20" length of 1"w white wired ribbon. Fold 2½" of one end of ribbon under to form first loop. Approximately 5" from folded end of first loop, fold ribbon over in opposite direction. Approximately 4½" from folded end of second loop, fold ribbon over in opposite direction to form third loop. Approximately 4" from folded end of third loop, fold ribbon over in opposite direction to form fourth loop. Hand sew at center front through all thicknesses of ribbon. Trim excess ribbon.

10. To make streamers, cut a 10" length of 1"w white wired ribbon. Matching centers, tie length around bow, placing knot at back of bow. Refer to Fig. 84 to fold and notch ends of streamers.

Fig. 84

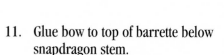

11. Glue bow to top of barrette below snapdragon stem.

12. Bend snapdragon stem into an arch to fit bridesmaid's head.

BRIDE'S BOUQUET

SUPPLIES

1³⁄₈" x 3½" bouquet holder
6" dia. lace bouquet collar
1⅝ yds — 2"w double-face satin ribbon
1⅓ yds — ⅞"w satin ribbon
3 large silk mums
1 small silk mum
5 satin leaf clusters
2 large bridal floral sprays
5 pearl stems
Hot glue gun and glue sticks (optional)
Thick, clear-drying craft glue
Craft scissors or wire cutters
Floral picks
Floral pins
Floral tape

Please familiarize yourself with basic techniques found in General Instructions, pg. 108, before beginning project. The measurements on the Placement Diagram indicate the length of the stem from the base of the flower or lowest leaf.

INSTRUCTIONS

1. Divide one large floral spray in half. Refer to Placement Diagram, pg. 72, for measurements and follow Preparing Flowers and Greenery, pg. 108, to separate, trim and wrap stems of all flowers (except remaining large bridal floral spray), leaves, and pearl stems. Use floral tape to join one pearl stem to each leaf cluster.

2. Insert handle of bouquet holder through center of bouquet collar; glue in place.

3. Refer to Placement Diagram to insert large mums and floral spray halves into bouquet holder.

4. To make bow, measure to a starting point 21" from one end of 2"w ribbon and hold ribbon at this point between thumb and forefinger. For first loop, measure 8" from starting point and fold ribbon to form a loop by matching starting point and second point.

Measure 8" from second point and form loop by matching second point and third point. Leave a 21" length of ribbon at the end of the second loop for streamer. Hand baste all loops and streamers together at the base of loops. Pull basting thread as tight as possible; secure and clip thread.

5. To make ribbon loop, measure to a starting point 21" from one end of ⅞"w ribbon and hold ribbon at this point between thumb and forefinger. For loop, measure 8" from starting point and fold ribbon to form a loop by matching starting point and second point. Leave an 18" length of ribbon at the end of the loop for streamer. Hand baste loop and streamers together at the base of loop. Pull basting thread as tight as possible; secure and clip thread.

6. Matching bases of loops, hand sew ribbon loop on top of bow. Refer to Assembling Bouquets, pg. 109, to insert floral pin in bow. Insert floral-pinned bow and loop into bouquet holder.

7. Refer to Placement Diagram to insert small mum and leaf clusters with pearl stems into bouquet holder.

8. Following Preparing Flowers and Greenery, pg. 108, separate and wrap cuttings from remaining floral spray together as desired. Insert cuttings into bouquet.

PLACEMENT DIAGRAM

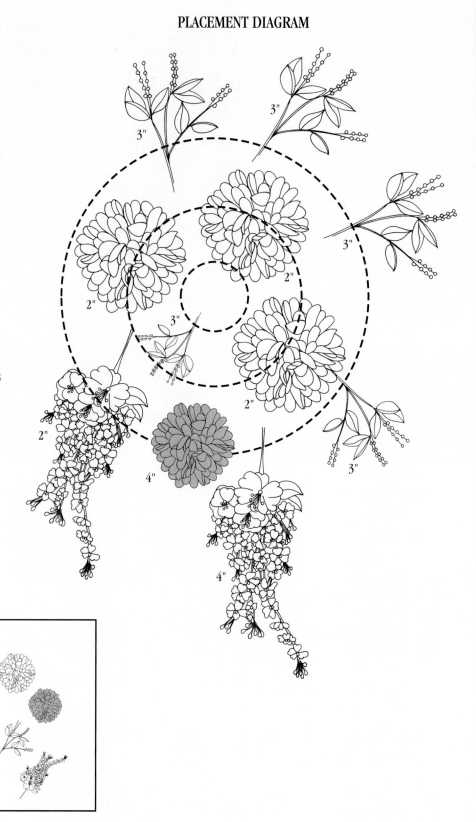

KEY

Large mum

Small mum

Leaf cluster

Floral spray

BRIDESMAID'S BOUQUET

SUPPLIES

1⅜" x 3½" bouquet holder
6½" lace bouquet collar
14" x 18" piece of silk or lightweight
   satin
1⅛ yds — 1½"w satin ribbon
½ yd — 1½"w variegated wired
   ribbon for rosettes
1 yd — ⅞"w satin ribbon
2 — 15" silk snapdragon stems
1 silk delphinium spray
1 small silk scilla spray
1 pkg pearl stamens
Hot glue gun and glue sticks
   (optional)
Thick, clear-drying craft glue
Craft scissors or wire cutters
Floral picks
Floral pins
Floral tape

Please familiarize yourself with basic techniques found in General Instructions, pg. 108, before beginning project. The measurements on the Placement Diagram indicate the length of the stem from the base of the flower or lowest leaf.

INSTRUCTIONS

1. Refer to Fig. 85 to trim one snapdragon to 10". Trim remaining snapdragon approximately 1" below lowest blossom. Follow Preparing Flowers and Greenery, pg. 108, to wrap stems.

Fig. 85

10"

2. Refer to Placement Diagram, pg. 74, for measurements and follow Preparing Flowers and Greenery, pg. 108, to separate, trim, and wrap three small delphiniums, one large delphinium, and one scilla from sprays. Trim two large delphiniums and two scillas from sprays close to base of each flower.

3. Insert handle of bouquet holder through center of bouquet collar; glue in place.

4. Refer to Placement Diagram to insert each snapdragon stem into bouquet holder. Bend each snapdragon stem.

5. For bow, fold long edges of silk ¾" to wrong side; press. Matching right sides and raw edges, fold silk in half. Lightly crease center. Pin and machine stitch ½" from raw edges; remove pins. Turn right side out; press seam. Matching seam to center crease, hand or machine baste along seam through all thicknesses. Pull basting threads as tight as possible; secure and clip thread. Refer to Assembling Bouquets, pg. 109, to insert floral pin through bow. Insert floral-pinned bow into bouquet holder.

6. To make ribbon loops, measure to a starting point 13" from one end of 1½"w ribbon and hold ribbon at this point between thumb and forefinger. For first loop, measure 6" from starting point and fold ribbon to form a loop by matching starting point and second point. Measure 6" from second point and form loop by matching second point and third point. Leave a 15½" length of ribbon at the end of the second loop for streamer. Hand baste all loops and streamers together at the base of loops. Pull basting thread as tight as possible; secure and clip thread.

7. To make additional ribbon loops, measure to a starting point 11" from one end of ⅞"w ribbon and hold ribbon at this point between thumb and forefinger. For first loop, measure 5" from starting point and fold ribbon to form a loop by matching starting point and second point. Measure 5" from second point and form loop by matching second point and third point. Leave a 13" length of ribbon at the end of the second loop for streamer. Hand baste all loops and streamers together at the base of loops. Pull basting thread as tight as possible; secure and clip thread.

PLACEMENT DIAGRAM

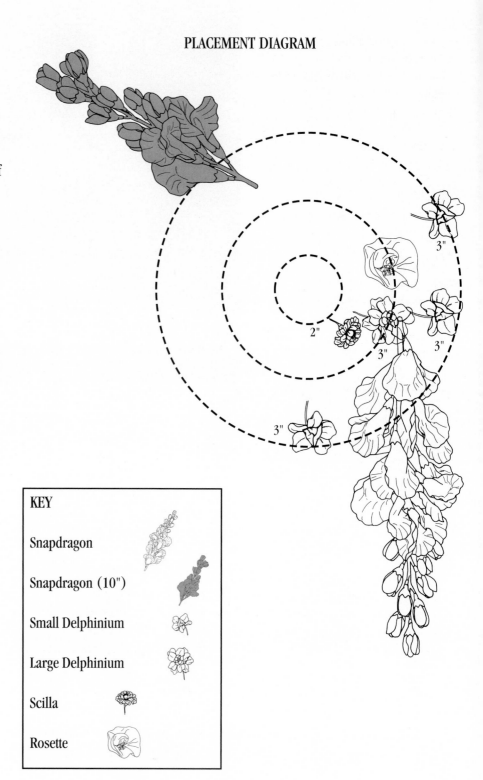

2"

3"

3"

3"

3"

KEY

Snapdragon

Snapdragon (10")

Small Delphinium

Large Delphinium

Scilla

Rosette

8. Refer to Assembling Bouquets, pg. 109, to insert floral pin through each loop. Insert floral-pinned loops into bouquet holder.

9. Refer to Placement Diagram, page 74, to insert wrapped delphiniums and wrapped scilla into bouquet holder. Glue remaining delphiniums and scillas on top of bow and loops.

10. To make rosettes, cut three 6" lengths of 1½"w wired ribbon. Hand baste ¼" from one long edge of one ribbon length. Pull basting thread as tight as possible; secure and clip thread. Fold one short edge of length at a 45° angle *(Fig. 86)*; hand sew bottom edges together. For center of rosette, keep edges even and turn point of ribbon to inside as shown in Fig. 87; hand sew edges together. Continue turning center of rosette to inside and hand sewing edges together. At end of ribbon fold remaining raw edge to back of rosette at a 45° angle; hand sew in place. Secure and clip thread. Repeat with remaining lengths of ribbon. Glue several pearl stamens to center of each rosette.

Fig. 86

Fig. 87

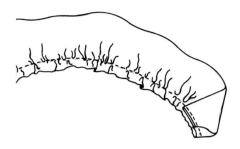

11. Refer to Assembling Bouquets, pg. 109, to insert floral pin through one rosette. Refer to Placement Diagram, pg. 74, and insert floral-pinned rosette into bouquet holder. Glue remaining rosettes on top of bow.

FLOWER GIRL'S HEADBAND
Photo, page 76

SUPPLIES
¼ yd — 44/45"w satin
½ yd elastic cord
Floral spray
Craft scissors or wire cutters

INSTRUCTIONS
1. For headband, cut a piece of satin 3½" x 28"; press short ends ½" to wrong side. Matching right sides and long edges, fold satin in half. Pin and stitch long edges together using ¼" seam allowance; turn satin right side out. Thread elastic cord through headband and tie in a knot to fit flower girl's head; trim ends of elastic. Insert one end of headband inside other end ¼"; hand sew together.

2. For rose, cut one 20" x 4" length of satin. Fold one short end of satin ½" to wrong side; press. Matching wrong sides and long edges, fold length in half. Do **not** press. Hand or machine baste ¼" from long raw edges. Pull basting thread as tight as possible; secure and clip thread. Fold short unpressed edges of length at a 45° angle *(Fig. 88)*; hand sew bottom edges together. For center of rose, keep raw edges even and turn point of length to inside as shown in Fig. 89; hand sew raw edges together. Continue turning center of rose to inside and hand sewing raw edges together. At end of length, secure and clip thread. Hand sew rose to center of headband on top of overlap.

Fig. 88

Fig. 89

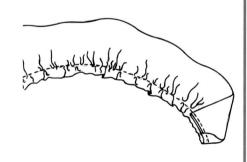

3. Hand sew clippings from floral spray to headband on each side of rose.

FLOWER GIRL'S BASKET

SUPPLIES
Small basket (3" dia. base)
⅜ yd — 44/45"w satin to line basket
⅜ yd — 44/45"w fleece
1 yd — 1"w variegated wired ribbon
   for rosettes
¾ yd — 1"w wired ribbon for large
   bows
1 yd — ⅜"w satin ribbon
Hot glue gun and glue sticks
3" circle of white poster board

INSTRUCTIONS
1. To determine size of fleece and satin, measure width and length of basket; add 6" to both measurements. Cut fleece and satin determined size.

2. Place fleece inside basket; trim excess fleece even with top edge if necessary.

3. With wrong side of satin next to fleece, place lining into basket on top of fleece.

4. For padded bottom, place poster board circle inside basket; trim to fit if necessary. Cut fleece same size as poster board; glue to poster board.

5. Cut satin for padded bottom 1¼" larger than poster board. Hand baste satin ¼" from raw edge. Center poster board, fleece side down, on wrong side of satin. Pull basting thread to gather fabric tightly around poster board; secure and clip thread. Glue gathered edge of satin to poster board.

6. Place padded bottom inside basket on top of satin.

7. Wrap satin over edges of basket, turning under raw edges and gluing in place as needed. Glue padded bottom to inside of basket.

8. Cut two 9" lengths of ⅜"w ribbon. Tie each ribbon length in a bow. Use remaining ⅜"w ribbon to wrap handle, gluing ends in place. Trim excess ribbon if necessary. Glue one bow to each side of basket where handle meets basket.

9. Cut 1"w ribbon for large bows in half. Tie each ribbon length in a bow. Glue one bow to each side of basket.

10. Refer to Fig. 90 to fold and notch ribbon ends.

Fig. 90

11. For each rosette, cut eight 4½" lengths of 1"w variegated ribbon. For each rosette, follow Step 2 of Radiance Bridesmaid's Shoes, pg. 78, to make each rosette. Glue two rosettes to basket on each side of large bows.

BRIDESMAID'S SHOES

SUPPLIES
1 pair dyed satin shoes
1 pair shoe clips
⅜ yd — 1¼"w variegated wired ribbon for rosettes
⅞ yd — ⅞"w satin ribbon
1 pkg pearl stamens
Hot glue gun and glue sticks

INSTRUCTIONS
1. For bows, cut ⅞"w ribbon in half. Fold 2½" of one end of one ribbon length under to form first loop. Approximately 3½" from folded end of first loop, fold ribbon over in opposite direction. Approximately 3¼" from folded end of second loop, fold ribbon over in opposite direction to form third loop. Approximately 3" from folded end of third loop, fold ribbon over in opposite direction to form fourth loop. Hand baste at center front through all thicknesses of ribbon. Pull basting thread as tight as possible; secure and clip thread. Trim excess ribbon if necessary. Repeat with remaining ribbon length.

2. For rosettes, cut 1¼"w wired ribbon in half. For each rosette, hand baste ¼" from one long edge of ribbon. Pull basting thread as tight as possible; secure and clip thread. Fold one short edge of length at a 45° angle *(Fig. 91)*; hand sew bottom edges together. For center of rosette, keep edges even and turn point of ribbon to inside as shown in Fig. 92; hand sew edges together. Continue turning center of rosette to inside and hand sewing edges together. At end of ribbon, fold remaining raw edge to back of rosette at a 45° angle; hand sew in place. Secure and clip thread.

Fig. 91

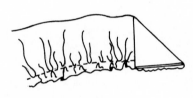

Fig. 92

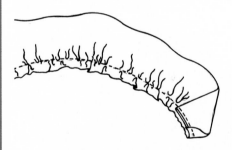

3. Glue several stamens to center of each rosette. Hand sew one rosette to each bow. Hand sew one bow to each shoe clip. Clip to toes of shoes.

BRIDE'S SHOES

SUPPLIES
1 pair satin shoes
1 pair shoe clips
2 floral rose sprays
Craft scissors or wire cutters

INSTRUCTIONS
1. Trim stem on each floral spray close to where all stems are taped together. Hand sew one floral spray to center of each shoe clip. Clip to toes of shoes.

GLOVES

SUPPLIES
1 pair long satin gloves
2 floral sprays
2 — 2½" x 8" pieces of satin
2 pkgs 4mm pearls
2 — 8mm pearls
Jewel glue
Craft scissors or wire cutters
Scrap paper

INSTRUCTIONS
1. Place scrap paper inside each glove. Glue 4mm pearls to gloves. Remove scrap paper.

2. For each rose, use one satin piece and fold one short end of satin ½" to wrong side; press. Matching wrong sides and long edges, fold length in half. Do **not** press. Hand or machine baste ¼" from long raw edges. Pull basting thread as tight as possible; secure and clip thread. Fold short unpressed edges of length at a 45° angle *(Fig. 93)*; hand sew bottom edges together. For center of rose, keep raw edges even and turn point of length to inside as shown in Fig. 94; hand sew raw edges together. Continue turning center of rose to inside and hand sewing raw edges together. At end of length, secure and clip thread. Glue one 8mm pearl in center of each rose.

Fig. 93

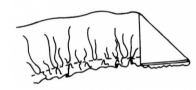

Fig. 94

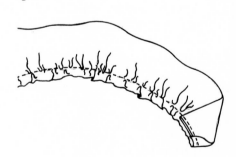

3. Trim stems on each floral spray close to where all stems are taped together. Hand sew one floral spray to top of each glove.

4. Glue one rose to center of each floral spray covering stem.

BRIDE'S VEIL

SUPPLIES
1 pearl headband
2 yds — 54"w tulle
7 yds — ¼"w satin ribbon
1 pkg Lily of the Valley and pearl spray (3 yd length)
4 pearl leaves
3" clear plastic hair comb
Hot glue gun and glue sticks

INSTRUCTIONS

1. For veil, cut one 1 yd length, one 27" length, and two 18" x 2½" pieces of tulle. Machine stitch ribbon to one long edge of each piece of tulle.

2. Hand or machine baste across width of 1 yd length of tulle 4" from ribbon. Hand or machine baste across width of 27" length of tulle 3" from ribbon. Pull basting thread on 1 yd length until gathers measure 7"; secure and clip threads. Repeat with 27" length.

3. Matching wrong sides and gathering lines, place the 27" length on top of the 1 yd length. Hand sew the two lengths together along gathering lines.

4. Cut an 18" length of ribbon. Glue one end of ribbon to one end of taped section of pearl headband. With edges of ribbon touching, but not overlapping, cover taped section by wrapping and gluing ribbon around taped section. Trim excess ribbon; glue end of ribbon to taped section of pearl headband.

5. With longest length on bottom, match centers and hand sew veil to back of pearl headband along gathering line.

6. To form rosette, hand or machine baste across one 18" x 2½" piece of tulle ¼" from long raw edge. Pull basting thread as tight as possible; secure and clip thread. Repeat with remaining piece of tulle. Glue one rosette to pearl headband on each side of veil.

7. To make ribbon loops, measure to a starting point 3" from one end of ribbon and hold ribbon at this point between thumb and forefinger. For first loop, measure 5" from starting point and fold ribbon to form a loop by matching starting point and second point. Measure 5" from second point and form loop by matching second point and third point. Continue forming loops in this manner until you have four loops. Leave a 3" length of ribbon at the end of the fourth loop for streamer. Hand baste all loops and streamers together at the base of loops. Refer to Fig. 95 to fold and notch ends of streamers. Repeat to make second set of ribbon loops.

Fig. 95

8. Glue ribbon loops to headband in front of rosettes. Glue pearl leaves to headband beside loops.

9. Cut four 6" lengths of Lily of the Valley and pearl spray. Fold each length in half to form a loop. Glue one pearl spray loop behind ribbon loops and glue one pearl spray loop under ribbon loops on each side.

10. Cut two 8" lengths of Lily of the Valley and pearl spray. Glue one length under ribbon loops on each side.

11. Working between teeth, use remaining ribbon to wrap top of comb. Use glue to secure ends of ribbon to comb.

12. Matching centers, hand sew comb to back of pearl headband underneath veil.

13. Bend pearl headband into a "V" shape at center front.

BRIDESMAID'S HAIR BOW

SUPPLIES
7½" x 16" piece of white satin
8½" x 16" piece of colored satin
½ yd — 1"w white satin ribbon
6" — ¼"w colored satin ribbon
1 pkg colored glass seed beads
2" barrette
3 small colored silk flowers
1 pkg pearl stamens
Hot glue gun and glue sticks
Beading needle

INSTRUCTIONS
(**Note**: *For all machine stitching, use a ¼" seam allowance. Backstitch at the beginning and end of each seam.*)

1. Leaving center and edges unbeaded, refer to Fig. 96 and use beading needle to sew beads to white satin.

Fig. 96

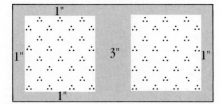

2. Matching right sides and long edges, pin and machine stitch white and colored satin pieces together along both long edges. Remove pins. Turn right side out; carefully press edges. Colored satin will extend to front of satin tube.

3. Matching short ends, fold satin tube in half; lightly crease center. Unfold satin tube. With beaded side down, place satin tube on work surface. Fold each short end to center, overlapping center crease by ½"; pin in place. Machine baste across center of satin tube, stitching through all layers. Remove pins. Pull basting thread tightly to gather satin tube into bow; secure and clip thread.

4. Cut a 5" length of 1"w white ribbon. Fold each raw edge under ½"; press. Wrap ribbon around center of bow. Overlap ends 1"; hand sew in place.

5. For rosettes, cut two 6" lengths of 1"w white ribbon. Hand baste ¼" from one long edge of one ribbon length. Pull basting thread until gathers measure 4½". Fold one short edge of length at a 45° angle *(Fig. 97)*; hand sew bottom edges together. For center of rosette,

keep edges even and turn point of ribbon to inside as shown in Fig. 98; hand sew edges together. Continue turning center of rosette to inside and hand sewing edges together. At end of ribbon, secure and clip thread. Repeat with remaining lengths of ribbon. Glue several stamens into center of each rosette.

Fig. 97

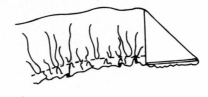

Fig. 98

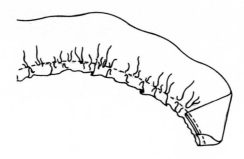

6. Glue rosettes to center of bow.

7. To form loops, cut three 2" lengths of ¼"w colored ribbon. Matching raw edges, fold each length in half. Glue loops behind rosettes.

8. Glue flowers between loops.

9. Matching centers, hand sew barrette to back of bow.

BRIDE'S BOUQUET

SUPPLIES

1⅜" x 3½" bouquet holder
4⅝ yds — 6"w tulle
1¼ yds — 3"w double-face satin ribbon
2⅝ yds — 2½"w double-face satin ribbon
2⅛ yds — 2"w striped ribbon
4⅝ yds — ¼"w satin ribbon
1 yd wired satin cord
3¼ yds — 6mm strung pearls
4 pearl cluster stamens
Hot glue gun and glue sticks (optional)
Thick, clear-drying craft glue
Floral pins

Please familiarize yourself with basic techniques found in General Instructions, pg. 108, before beginning project. The measurements on the Placement Diagram indicate the length of the stem from the base of the flower, lowest leaf, or base of pearl loop.

INSTRUCTIONS

1. Machine stitch ¼"w ribbon to one long edge of tulle.

2. Cut one 1⅝ yard length of tulle. Machine baste tulle ¼" from long raw edge. Pull basting thread until gathers measure 9"; secure and clip thread. Glue tulle to foam sides of bouquet holder along gathering line.

3. Baste remaining tulle ¼" from long raw edge. Pull basting thread until gathers measure 12"; secure and clip thread. Glue tulle to bouquet holder on top of first layer of tulle.

4. To make white bow, measure to a starting point 16½" from one end of 2½"w ribbon and hold ribbon at this point between thumb and forefinger. For first loop, measure 12" from starting point and fold ribbon to form a loop by matching starting point and second point. Measure 12" from second point and form loop by matching second point and third point. Leave a 16½" length of ribbon at the end of the second loop for streamer. Hand baste all loops and streamers together at the base of loops. Pull basting thread as tight as possible; secure and clip thread. Refer to Assembling Bouquets, pg. 109, to insert floral pin in bow. Insert floral-pinned bow into bouquet holder.

5. Cut one 32" length of striped ribbon. Matching raw edges, fold ribbon in half. Refer to Assembling Bouquets, pg. 109, to insert floral pin in fold of ribbon. Insert floral-pinned fold of ribbon into bouquet holder under bow.

6. Cut one 30" length, one 28" length, and one 24" length of strung pearls. Fold each length in half to form a loop; secure ends by wrapping with thread. Refer to Assembling Bouquets, pg. 109, to place floral pins over thread on pearl loops. Insert floral-pinned pearl loops into bouquet holder above center of bow.

7. To make large roses, cut two 22½" lengths of 3"w ribbon. Fold short ends of one ribbon at a 45° angle. Hand or machine baste length along longest edge. Pull basting thread as tight as possible; secure and clip thread. Begin with one short end of length and loosely roll ¼" to inside, keeping bottom edges even. Hand sew bottom edges together. Continue rolling ribbon and hand sewing bottom edges together. At end of length, secure and clip thread. Repeat with remaining length of ribbon. Glue pearl cluster stamen to center of each rose.

8. For small roses, cut one 22½" length and one 13½" length of 2½"w ribbon. Follow Step 7 to make roses.

9. Refer to Assembling Bouquets, pg. 109, to insert floral pin in each rose. Refer to Placement Diagram to insert floral-pinned roses into bouquet holder.

10. Cut two 10" lengths and four 6" lengths of striped ribbon. Match raw edges of one length to form loop; secure ends by wrapping with thread. Repeat with remaining lengths. Refer to Assembling Bouquets, pg. 109, to insert floral pin in each loop. Insert floral-pinned loops into bouquet holder on top of bow.

11. Cut five 7" lengths of wired satin cord. Match raw edges of one length to form loop; secure ends by wrapping with thread. Repeat with remaining lengths. Cut five 7" lengths of pearls. Glue pearls to satin cord loops. Refer to Assembling Bouquets, pg. 109, to place floral pins over thread on loops. Insert floral-pinned loops into bouquet holder.

PLACEMENT DIAGRAM

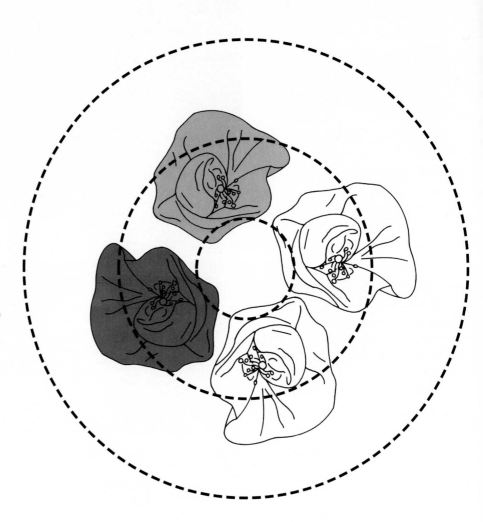

KEY	
3"w ribbon rose	
2½"w ribbon rose (22½" length)	
2½"w ribbon rose (13½" length)	

BRIDESMAID'S BOUQUET

SUPPLIES

1⅜" x 3½" plastic bouquet holder

3 yds — 6"w white tulle

1 yd — 1½"w colored double-face
   satin ribbon

1⅔ yds — ⅞"w white striped satin
   ribbon

1⅜ yds — ⅝"w colored satin ribbon

1⅝ yds — ⅜"w colored satin ribbon

3 yds — ¼"w colored satin ribbon to
   edge tulle

⅝ yd — ¼"w colored satin ribbon

1 lilac spray

1 pkg pearl stamens

1 yd — 6mm strung pearls

6" — 3mm strung pearls

Hot glue gun and glue sticks
   (optional)

Thick, clear-drying craft glue

Craft scissors or wire cutters

Floral picks

Floral pins

Floral tape

Please familiarize yourself with basic techniques found in General Instructions, pg. 108, before beginning project. The measurements on the Placement Diagram indicate the length of the stem from the base of the flower, lowest leaf, or base of pearl loop.

INSTRUCTIONS

1. Refer to Placement Diagram, pg. 87, for measurements and follow Preparing Flowers and Greenery, pg. 108, to separate, trim, and wrap stems of lilac spray.

2. Machine stitch ¼"w ribbon to one long edge of tulle.

3. Fold long, raw edge of tulle 1½" to wrong side. Machine baste through both layers of tulle ¼" from folded edge. Run another basting thread ⅛" from first basting thread. Pull both basting threads until gathers measure 10"; secure and clip threads.

4. With ribbon-edged portion of tulle to the front, refer to Fig. 99 and glue tulle around foam center of bouquet holder along gathering lines.

Fig. 99

5. To make striped bow, measure to a starting point 12" from one end of striped ribbon and hold ribbon at this point between thumb and forefinger. For first loop, measure 12" from starting point and fold ribbon to form a loop by matching starting point and second point. Measure 12" from second point and form loop by matching second point and third point. Leave a 12" length of ribbon at the end of the second loop for streamer. Hand baste all loops and streamers together at the base of loops.

6. To make colored bow, measure to a starting point 13½" from one end of ⅝"w ribbon and hold ribbon at this point between thumb and forefinger. For first loop, measure 10" from starting point and fold ribbon to form a loop by matching starting point and second point. Measure 10" from second point and form loop by matching second point and third point. Leave a 12½" length of ribbon at the end of the second loop for streamer. Hand baste all loops and streamers together at the base of loops.

7. To make additional colored bow, follow Step 6 using ⅜"w ribbon.

8. Cut a 4" length of ¼"w colored ribbon. Matching centers of all bows, tie ¼"w ribbon around bows, placing knot at back of bows. Trim ends of ¼"w ribbon close to knot. Refer to Assembling Bouquets, pg. 109, to insert floral pin through bow. Insert floral-pinned bow into bouquet holder.

9. Cut one 16" length and one 20" length of 6mm strung pearls. Fold each length in half to form a loop; secure ends by wrapping with thread. Refer to Assembling Bouquets, pg. 109, to insert floral pin over thread on pearl loop. Insert floral-pinned loops into bouquet holder.

10. For rosettes, cut three 11" lengths of 1½"w ribbon. Hand baste ¼" from long edge of one ribbon length. Pull basting thread as tight as possible; secure and clip thread. Fold one short edge of length at a 45° angle *(Fig. 100)*; hand sew bottom edges together. For center of rosette, keep edges even and turn point of ribbon to inside as shown in Fig. 101; hand sew edges together. Continue turning center of rosette to inside and hand sewing edges together. At end of ribbon, fold remaining raw edge to back of rosette at a 45° angle; hand sew in place. Secure and clip thread. Repeat with remaining lengths of ribbon. Glue several pearl stamens to center of each rosette.

Fig. 100

Fig. 101

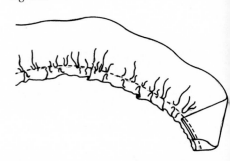

11. Refer to Assembling Bouquets, pg. 109, to insert floral pin through each rosette. Refer to Placement Diagram, pg. 87, for placement of rosettes and insert floral-pinned rosettes into bouquet holder.

12. Refer to Placement Diagram, pg. 87, to insert each lilac stem into bouquet holder.

13. Cut remaining striped ribbon and ⅜"w ribbon in half. Matching raw edges, fold each length in half to form a loop; secure ends by wrapping with thread.

14. Cut four 4" lengths of remaining ¼"w ribbon. Matching raw edges, fold each length in half to form a loop; secure ends by wrapping with thread.

15. Cut 3mm strung pearls in half. Fold each length in half to form a loop; secure ends by wrapping with thread.

16. Refer to Assembling Bouquets, pg. 109, to insert floral pin through each ribbon loop and over thread on each pearl loop. Insert floral-pinned ribbon loops and pearl loops into bouquet holder.

Fig. 102

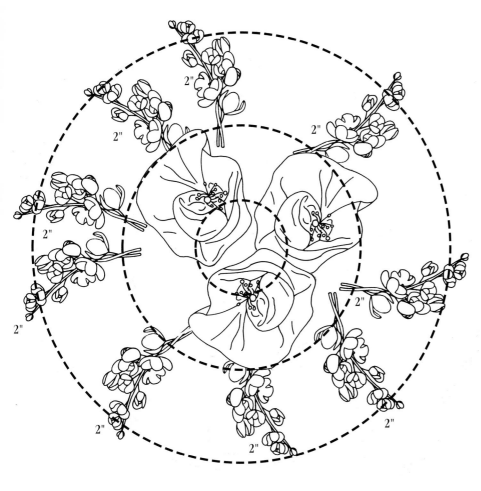

PLACEMENT DIAGRAM

2. For each glove, cut a 2" length of pearls. Glue pearls around center of each bow. Hand sew a bow to each glove.

3. Cut two 13½" lengths of pearls. Fold each length in half; secure ends by wrapping with thread. Bring center of folded length to wrapped ends, forming two loops; secure by wrapping with thread. Hand sew wrapped portion of loops to each glove right below bow.

RING BEARER'S PILLOW
Photo, page 89

SUPPLIES
10" x 12" piece of white satin
10" x 12" piece of colored satin
⅞ yd — 1½"w double-face white satin ribbon
2 — 1 yd lengths of ¼"w colored satin ribbon (two colors)
1⅛ yds — ¼"w white satin ribbon
Polyester fiberfill
1 pkg colored glass seed beads
4 — 2½" colored silk lilac stems
1 pkg pearl stamens
Jewel glue

INSTRUCTIONS
1. For pillow, match right sides and raw edges of satin pieces. Leaving an opening for turning, pin and stitch pieces together using ½" seam allowance. Trim seam allowances to ¼" and clip corners. Turn pillow right side out; press.

GLOVES
Photo, page 89

SUPPLIES
1 pair short satin gloves
1 yd — 2"w striped ribbon
1 yd — 6mm strung pearls
Hot glue gun and glue sticks

INSTRUCTIONS
1. Cut ribbon in half. Tie each ribbon length in a bow. Refer to Fig. 102 to fold and notch ribbon ends.

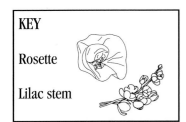

KEY

Rosette

Lilac stem

87

2. Lightly stuff pillow with fiberfill. Hand sew opening closed.

3. Cut a 21" length of 1½"w ribbon. Matching raw edges, fold length in half. Hand or machine baste through both layers 3" from raw edges. Pull basting thread until gathers measure ¾"; secure and clip thread. Refer to Fig. 103 to fold and notch ribbon ends.

Fig. 103

4. With notched ribbon ends facing up, slide ribbon loop over pillow.

5. For colored ribbon loops, match raw edges and fold one ¼"w colored ribbon length in half. Measure 2" from fold and hand sew this point to gathering line of 1½"w ribbon. Repeat with remaining ¼"w colored ribbon length.

6. For rosettes, cut remaining 1½"w ribbon in half. Hand baste ¼" from one long edge of ribbon. Pull basting thread as tight as possible; secure and clip thread. Fold one short edge of length at a 45° angle *(Fig. 104)*; hand sew bottom edges together. For center of rosette, keep edges even and turn point of ribbon to inside as shown in Fig. 105; hand sew edges together. Continue turning center of rosette to inside and hand sew edges together. At end of ribbon, fold remaining raw edge to back of rosette at a 45° angle; hand sew in place. Secure and clip thread.

Fig. 104

Fig. 105

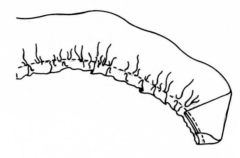

7. Glue several stamens to center of each rosette. Hand sew rosettes on top of ribbon loops.

8. Tie ¼"w white ribbon in a bow. Hand sew bow to ribbon loops below rosettes. Trim all ribbon ends as desired.

9. Glue lilacs behind rosettes and ribbon loops.

10. Glue beads to pillow.

BRIDESMAID'S SHOES

SUPPLIES

1 pair dyed satin shoes
1 pair shoe clips
2 — 2" x 8" pieces of white satin
2 — 2½" x 8" pieces of colored satin
⅓ yd — ⅝"w white satin ribbon
⅛ yd — ⅛"w white satin ribbon
1 pkg colored glass seed beads
2 small colored silk blossoms
Jewel glue

INSTRUCTIONS

1. For each bow, match right sides and long edges of one white satin piece and one colored satin piece; pin and stitch along both long edges using ¼" seam allowance. Turn right side out; carefully press edges. Colored satin will extend to front of satin tube.

2. Matching short ends, fold satin tube in half; lightly crease center. Unfold satin tube. With white satin side down, place satin tube on work surface. Fold each short end to center, overlapping center crease by ½"; pin in place. Machine baste across center of satin tube, stitching through all layers. Pull basting thread as tight as possible to gather satin tube into bow; secure and clip thread.

3. Cut ⅛"w ribbon in half. Wrap one length of ribbon around center of each bow; overlap ends and hand sew to back of each bow.

4. For rosettes, cut four 3" lengths of ⅝"w ribbon. Follow Step 6 of Ribbon Fantasy Ring Bearer's Pillow, this page, to make each rosette. Glue two rosettes to center of each bow. Glue blossoms above rosettes.

5. Glue beads to bows.

6. Hand sew one bow to each shoe clip. Clip to toes of shoes.

BRIDE'S HAT

SUPPLIES
- 24" dia. doily
- 2 — 8" dia. doilies
- 2 — 6" dia. doilies
- 2½ yds — 3"w satin ribbon
- 6" — ¼"w satin ribbon
- 1 large silk rose
- 2 small rose sprays
- 2 pearl loops
- Fabric stiffener
- Bowl (to fit bride's head)
- Aluminum foil
- Hot glue gun and glue sticks

INSTRUCTIONS
1. Cover outside of bowl with foil. Set bowl, bottom up, on a sheet of foil, making sure foil sheet is larger than the 24" doily (piece if necessary).

2. Follow manufacturer's instructions to apply fabric stiffener to 24" doily. Center doily on foil-covered bowl and carefully drape and mold doily over bowl. Let dry 24 hours; carefully remove hat from foil-covered bowl.

3. Apply fabric stiffener to remaining doilies; place on foil sheet until almost dry. To form damp doilies into roses, hold center of doily between fingers and gently twist doily *(Fig. 106)*. Shape petals as desired. Allow roses to dry completely.

Fig. 106

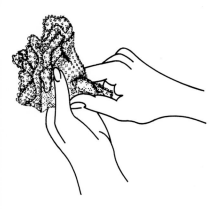

4. To make bow loops, cut two 10" lengths from 3"w ribbon. Matching raw edges, fold one length in half. Hand or machine baste ¼" from raw edges. Gather ends to measure 1" *(Fig. 107)*; secure and clip thread. Repeat with remaining 10" length of ribbon.

Fig. 107

5. Position center of remaining 3"w ribbon on hat crown right above brim. Refer to Fig. 108 to thread ¼"w ribbon through hat and over 3"w ribbon. Tie ¼"w ribbon in a knot inside hat, gathering 3"w ribbon; trim ribbon ends close to knot. This will be center front of hat. Draw ribbon around crown of hat and tie in a knot at center back of hat.

Fig. 108

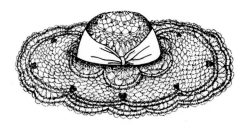

6. Refer to Fig.109 to fold and notch ends of ribbon.

Fig. 109

7. Glue large silk rose to center back of hat over ribbon knot. Refer to Fig. 110 for placement and glue rose sprays and doily roses to hat.

Fig. 110

8. Glue bow loops and pearl loops to hat behind large silk rose.

BRIDESMAID'S HAT
Photos, page 92

SUPPLIES
24" dia. doily
2 — 8" dia. doilies
⅔ yd — 3"w white satin ribbon
2 yds — 1⅝"w white satin ribbon
2 yds — 1"w colored satin ribbon
½ yd — ⅝"w colored satin ribbon
6" — ¼"w colored satin ribbon
3 large colored silk carnations
2 small colored silk rose sprays
2 ivy stems
Fabric stiffener
Bowl (to fit bridesmaid's head)
Aluminum foil
Hot glue gun and glue sticks

INSTRUCTIONS
1. Cover outside of bowl with foil. Set bowl, bottom up, on a sheet of foil, making sure foil sheet is larger than the 24" doily (piece if necessary).

2. Follow manufacturer's instructions to apply fabric stiffener to 24" doily. Center doily on foil-covered bowl and carefully drape and mold doily over bowl. Let dry 24 hours; carefully remove hat from foil-covered bowl.

3. Apply fabric stiffener to remaining doilies; place on foil sheet until almost dry. To form damp doilies into roses, hold center of doily between finger and gently twist doily *(Fig. 111)*. Shape petals as desired. Allow roses to dry completely.

Fig. 111

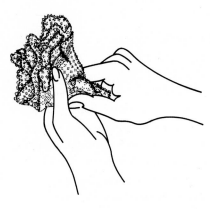

4. Cut an 18" length of 1⅝"w ribbon. Center ⅝"w ribbon length on top of 1⅝"w ribbon length. Holding ribbons together and matching short ends, fold in half; lightly crease centers. Position center of ribbons on hat crown right above brim. Refer to Fig. 112 to thread ¼"w ribbon through hat and over ribbons; tie ¼"w ribbon in a knot inside hat, gathering ribbons; trim ¼"w ribbon ends close to knot. This will be center front of hat. Drape ribbons around crown of hat and glue ribbon ends to center back of hat.

Fig. 112

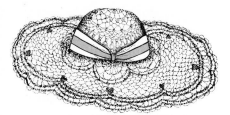

5. Refer to photo to fold brim of hat to crown; hand sew in place.

6. Refer to Fig. 113 to glue ivy, rose sprays, and doily roses around brim of hat.

Fig. 113

7. To make bow loops, cut 3"w ribbon in half. Matching raw edges, fold one length in half. Baste ¼" from raw edges. Gather ends to measure 1" *(Fig. 114);* secure and clip thread. Repeat with remaining length of ribbon. Glue loops under folded edge of hat brim.

Fig. 114

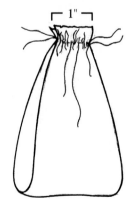

8. For white streamers, cut remaining 1⅝"w ribbon in half. Glue streamers to hat on top of folded edge of hat brim.

9. For bow, measure to a starting point 21" from one end of 1"w ribbon and hold ribbon at this point between thumb and forefinger. For first loop, measure 6" from starting point and fold ribbon to form a loop by matching starting point and second point. Measure 6" from second point and form loop by matching second point and third point. Continue forming loops in this manner until you have four loops. Leave a 21" length of ribbon at the end of the fourth loop for streamer. Hand baste all loops and streamers together at the base of loops.

10. Glue bow to back of hat on top of white streamers.

11. Refer to Fig. 115 to fold and notch all ribbon ends.

Fig. 115

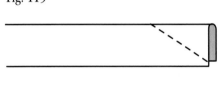

12. Glue carnations on top of bow.

BRIDE'S BOUQUET
Photo, page 94

SUPPLIES

1⅜" x 3½" bouquet holder
9" dia. lace bouquet collar
12" dia. doily
1½ yds — 1½"w white double-face satin ribbon
1½ yds — ⅞"w colored satin ribbon
2 large white silk roses
2 white silk rosebud sprays
3 silk carnations (1 white and 2 colored)
2 colored silk sweet pea stems with buds
1 bunch ivy
4 large pearl sprays
Fabric stiffener
Hot glue gun and glue sticks (optional)
Thick, clear-drying craft glue
Craft scissors or wire cutters
Floral picks
Floral pins
Floral tape

Please familiarize yourself with basic techniques found in General Instructions, pg. 108, before beginning project. The measurements on the Placement Diagram indicate the length of the stem from the base of the flower or lowest leaf.

INSTRUCTIONS

1. Refer to Placement Diagram, page 95, for measurements and follow Preparing Flowers and Greenery, pg. 108, to separate, trim, and wrap stems of all flowers and pearl sprays.

2. Follow manufacturer's instructions to apply fabric stiffener to doily. Let doily dry 24 hours. Cut a 2" dia. hole in center of doily. Insert handle of bouquet holder through hole in doily.

3. Insert handle of bouquet holder through center of bouquet collar. Glue collar and doily to bouquet holder.

4. To make white bow, measure to a starting point 15" from one end of 1½"w ribbon and hold ribbon at this point between thumb and forefinger. For first loop, measure 10" from starting point and fold ribbon to form a loop by matching starting point and second point. Measure 10" from second point and form loop by matching second point and third point. Leave a 15" length of ribbon at the end of the second loop for streamer. Hand baste all loops and streamers together at the base of loops. Pull basting thread as tight as possible; secure and clip thread.

5. Repeat Step 4, using ⅞"w colored ribbon.

6. Refer to Placement Diagram, page 95, to insert roses, rosebuds, carnations, and sweet peas into bouquet holder.

7. Refer to Assembling Bouquets, pg. 109, to insert floral pin into white bow. Insert floral-pinned bow into bouquet holder. Matching centers, glue colored bow on top of white bow.

8. Following Preparing Flowers and Greenery, pg. 108, separate and wrap ivy. Insert ivy and pearl sprays into bouquet.

PLACEMENT DIAGRAM

3½"
4"
4"
3"
4"
4½"
3"
3"
3½"
3"
5"
3"
4"
4"
2"
3"
4"
4"
2"
3"
3"
3"
5"
4"
3"
3½"
4½"

KEY

Rose

Rosebud

Double rosebud

Carnation

Colored carnation

Sweet pea

Sweet pea bud

BRIDESMAID'S BOUQUET
Photo, page 96

SUPPLIES
  1⅜" x 3½" bouquet holder
  6½" dia. lace bouquet collar
  10" dia. doily
  3 — 4" dia. doilies
  3¾ yds — ⅞"w satin ribbon
  ⅔ yd — ⅝"w satin ribbon
  3 large silk carnations
  7 silk rosebuds
  1 bunch ivy
  Fabric stiffener
  Hot glue gun and glue sticks
    (optional)
  Thick, clear-drying craft glue
  Craft scissors or wire cutters
  Floral picks
  Floral pins
  Floral tape

Please familiarize yourself with basic techniques found in General Instructions, pg. 108, before beginning project. The measurements on the Placement Diagram indicate the length of the stem from the base of the flower or lowest leaf.

INSTRUCTIONS
1. Refer to Placement Diagram, page 97, for measurements and follow Preparing Flowers and Greenery, pg. 108, to separate, trim, and wrap stems of all flowers.

2. Follow manufacturer's instructions to apply fabric stiffener to 10" doily. Let doily dry 24 hours. Cut a 2" dia. hole in center of doily. Insert handle of bouquet holder through hole in doily.

3. Insert handle of bouquet holder through center of bouquet collar. Glue collar and doily to bouquet holder.

4. Refer to Placement Diagram, page 97, to insert carnations and rosebuds into bouquet holder.

5. Gather center of each 4" doily between fingers as shown in Fig. 116; hand sew gathers together. Refer to Assembling Bouquets, pg. 109, to insert floral pin through each doily. Insert floral-pinned doilies into bouquet holder.

Fig. 116

6. To make ribbon loops, cut four 6" lengths of ⅝"w ribbon and two 8" lengths of ⅞"w ribbon. Matching raw edges, fold one length in half to form a loop; secure ends by wrapping with thread. Repeat with remaining ribbon lengths.

7. For bows, cut remaining ⅞"w ribbon in half. Measure to a starting point 19" from one end of one length of ribbon and hold ribbon at this point between thumb and forefinger. For first loop, measure 6" from starting point and fold ribbon to form a loop by matching starting point and second point. Measure 6"

from second point and form loop by matching second point and third point. Measure 6" from third point and form loop by matching third point and fourth point. Leave remaining ribbon at the end of the third loop for streamer. Hand baste all loops and streamers together at the base of loops. Pull basting thread as tight as possible; secure and clip thread. Repeat with remaining length of ribbon.

8. Refer to Assembling Bouquets, pg. 109, to insert floral pin through each bow and ribbon loop. Insert floral-pinned bows and loops into bouquet holder.

9. Following Preparing Flowers and Greenery, pg. 108, separate and wrap ivy. Insert ivy into bouquet holder.

PLACEMENT DIAGRAM

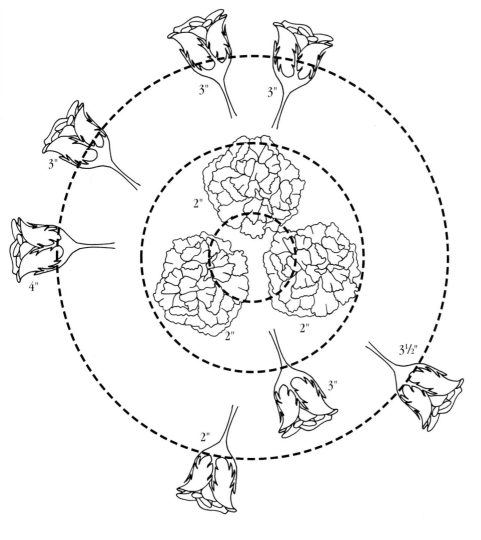

3" 3"

3"

2"

4"

3½"

2" 2"

2"

3"

2"

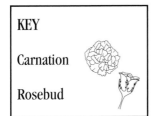

KEY

Carnation

Rosebud

BRIDESMAID'S SHOES
Photo, page 99

SUPPLIES
1 pair dyed satin shoes
2 — 4" heart-shaped doilies
1¾ yds — ⅝"w colored satin ribbon
6 —10mm pearls
Fabric stiffener
Hot glue gun and glue sticks
Jewel glue

INSTRUCTIONS
1. Measure 1½" from point at bottom of one heart-shaped doily; mark with pin. Hand baste from center top of doily to pin *(Fig. 117)*. Pull basting thread as tight as possible to gather doily; secure and clip thread. Repeat with remaining doily.

Fig. 117

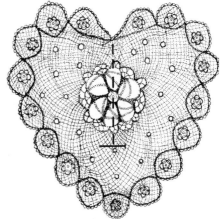

2. Follow manufacturer's instructions to apply fabric stiffener to top half of doilies. Let dry 24 hours.

3. For each shoe, use jewel glue to attach lower half of doily to shoe.

4. To make ribbon loops, cut thirty 2" lengths of ⅝"w ribbon. Matching raw edges, fold each ribbon length in half; secure ends by wrapping with thread.

5. Hot glue fifteen ribbon loops in layers on top of doily, forming a flower-like effect on one shoe. Hot glue three pearls to center of ribbon loops. Repeat with remaining shoe, ribbon loops, and pearls.

GLOVES
Photo, page 99

SUPPLIES
1 pair short crocheted gloves
6" dia. doily
¾ yd — ⅞"w colored satin ribbon
1 yd — ⅛"w colored satin ribbon
Fray Check™

INSTRUCTIONS
1. Cut ⅛"w ribbon in half. Beginning and ending at center front, loosely weave one ribbon length through each glove at wrist. Tie ends together in a bow; trim ends if necessary.

2. Cut doily in half; apply Fray Check to cut edges; allow to dry. Hand baste each doily half ¼" from cut edge. Pull basting threads until gathers measure 1"; secure and clip threads. Hand sew gathered edge of one doily half to each glove.

3. Cut two 9" lengths of ⅞"w ribbon. Tie each ribbon length in a bow. Hand sew one bow to each glove on top of doily. Refer to Fig. 118 to fold and notch ribbon ends.

Fig. 118

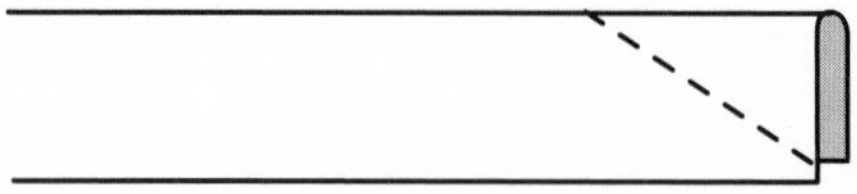

4. For rosettes, cut two 3½" lengths of ⅞"w ribbon. Hand baste ½" from one long edge of each ribbon length. Pull basting threads as tight as possible; secure and clip threads. Hand sew one rosette to center of each bow.

BRIDE'S BAG
Photo, page 99

SUPPLIES
2 — 10" heart-shaped doilies
¼ yd — 44/45"w colored fabric for lining
1 yd — ⅞"w colored satin ribbon
1½ yds — ⅛"w colored satin ribbon
1¼ yds — 3mm colored strung pearls
Hot glue gun and glue sticks
Tracing paper

INSTRUCTIONS
1. For lining, use pencil and tracing paper to trace doily shape as shown by shaded area in Fig. 119. Add ¾" across top of traced pattern and ½" to sides and bottom; cut out traced pattern. Cut out two fabric shapes.

Fig. 119

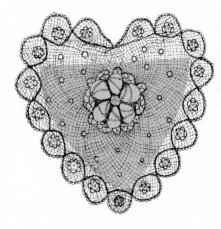

2. Matching **wrong** sides and raw edges, pin and stitch fabric shapes along sides and bottom using ¼" seam allowance. Trim seam allowances to ⅛". Turn shape wrong side out; press. Stitch ¼" from pressed edge.

3. To hem top edge, press raw edges ¼" to wrong side; press ½" to wrong side again. Stitch close to first fold; turn lining right side out.

4. Matching wrong sides and scalloped edges, pin doilies together. Leaving rounded tops of doilies unstitched, stitch sides and bottom together just inside scallops *(Fig. 120)*.

Fig. 120

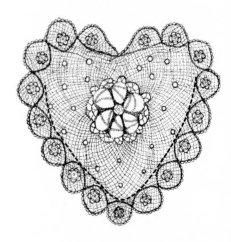

5. Insert lining into doily bag. Hand sew top edge of lining to doily bag.

6. For drawstrings, cut ⅛"w ribbon in half. Beginning and ending at center front, weave one ribbon length through doily bag right above lining; tie ends together in an overhand knot. Beginning and ending at center back, repeat with remaining ribbon length.

7. Cut a single pearl from strung pearls for each scallop on doily bag below drawstrings. Glue one pearl to each scallop.

8. For pearl loops, cut one 7", one 8", one 9", and one 10" length of pearls. Fold each length in half; secure ends by wrapping with thread. Glue wrapped ends of each pearl loop to center front of bag ½" below drawstrings.

9. For bow, measure to a starting point 4½" from one end of ⅞"w ribbon and hold ribbon at this point between thumb and forefinger. For first loop, measure 5" from starting point and fold ribbon to form a loop by matching starting point and second point. Measure 5" from second point and form loop by matching second point and third point. Continue forming loops in this manner until you have four loops. Leave a 4½" length of ribbon at the end of the fourth loop for streamer. Hand baste all loops and streamers together at the base of loops. Pull basting

thread as tight as possible; secure and clip thread. Cut two 2" lengths of pearls. Wrap pearl lengths around center of bow; glue ends to back of bow. Glue bow to center front of doily bag on top of pearl loops.

10. Refer to Fig. 121 to fold and notch ribbon ends.

Fig. 121

Victorian Romance

BRIDE'S VEIL

SUPPLIES

- 1½ yds — 54"w tulle
- ½ yd — ⅝"w braided trim
- ⅞ yd — 2¼"w satin ribbon
- ⅞ yd — ¼"w satin ribbon
- ½ yd — 2¾"w flat lace (with one straight edge)
- 1 pkg Lily of the Valley and pearl spray (3 yd length)
- White or clear plastic headband
- 3" clear plastic hair comb
- Hot glue gun and glue sticks

INSTRUCTIONS

1. To make veil, refer to Fig. 122 to fold tulle. To form pouf, hand or machine baste across width of veil 6" from folded edge. Run another basting thread ¼" from first basting thread. Pull both basting threads until gathers measure 8"; secure and clip threads.

Fig. 122

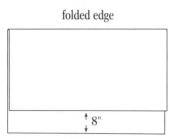

folded edge

8"

2. With pouf on top, match centers and glue veil to one outer edge of headband.

3. Fold raw edges of 2¼"w ribbon as shown in Fig. 123. Hand or machine baste ribbon along longest edge. Pull basting thread until gathers measure 9"; secure and clip threads. Matching

centers, glue gathered edge of ribbon to headband in front of veil.

Fig. 123

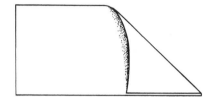

4. Glue braided trim to headband in front of ribbon.

5. Fold raw edges of lace ½" to wrong side. Hand or machine baste lace along long straight edge. Pull basting thread until gathers measure 8"; secure and clip threads. Matching centers, glue lace to headband between ribbon and veil.

6. Cut one 15" and two 13" lengths of Lily of the Valley and pearl spray. Glue one end of all three lengths of spray to center of headband between pouf and short layer of veil, with 15" length in the center.

7. Cut four 4½" lengths of Lily of the Valley and pearl spray. Glue sprays to headband, lace, and veil as desired.

8. For bows, cut two 8" lengths of ¼"w ribbon and tie each length in a bow; trim ends as desired. Glue bows to headband in front of 2¼"w ribbon as desired.

9. Working between teeth, use remaining ¼"w ribbon to wrap top of comb. Use glue to secure ends of ribbon to comb.

10. Matching centers, hand sew comb to veil behind headband.

BRIDESMAID'S HAIR BOW

SUPPLIES
4" x 2" oval barrette kit to cover
6" x 4" piece of satin
1½ yds — 1½"w wired ribbon
⅓ yd — 1"w satin ribbon
1 pkg Lily of the Valley and pearl spray (3 yd length)
1 yd — 3mm strung pearls
1 silk rose
Hot glue gun and glue sticks

INSTRUCTIONS
1. Follow manufacturer's instructions to cover barrette with satin.

2. For bow, cut a 40" length of 1½"w wired ribbon. Measure to a starting point 8" from one end and hold ribbon at this point between thumb and forefinger. For first loop, measure 6" from starting point and fold ribbon to form a loop by matching starting point and second point.

Measure 6" from second point and form loop by matching second point and third point. Continue forming loops in this manner until you have four loops. Leave an 8" length of ribbon at the end of the fourth loop for streamer. Hand baste all loops and streamers together at the base of loops.

3. For additional streamer, cut a 9" length of 1½"w wired ribbon. Glue one end of streamer to center back of bow. Refer to Fig. 124 to fold and notch ends of all streamers. Glue bow to center front of barrette.

Fig. 124

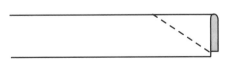

4. To make additional bow loops, cut 1"w satin ribbon in half. Matching raw edges, fold one length in half. Baste ¼" from raw edges. Tightly gather ends *(Fig. 125);* secure and clip thread. Repeat with remaining length of ribbon. Glue satin loops to barrette between wired ribbon bow loops.

Fig. 125

5. For pearl loops, cut one 13" length, one 11½" length, and one 10" length of pearls. Fold each length in half to form a loop; glue ends to center of bow.

6. Glue rose to center of bow on top of pearl loops.

7. Cut four 6" lengths of Lily of the Valley and pearl spray. Fold each length in half to form a loop. Glue ends of pearl loops between ribbon loops. Cut three 8" lengths of Lily of the Valley and pearl spray. Glue one end of each length under rose.

BRIDE'S BOUQUET

SUPPLIES

1⅜" x 3½" bouquet holder
9" dia. lace bouquet collar
1⅛ yds — 1"w white picot-edge ribbon
1¼ yds — 1"w white striped ribbon
1⅝ yds — ⅞"w colored ribbon
2 large colored silk roses with leaves
3 colored silk rosebuds with leaves
5 white silk lilac clusters
4 white bayberry clusters with leaves
5 white tiny berry clusters
6 white berry willow stem triple clusters
Hot glue gun and glue sticks (optional)
Thick, clear-drying craft glue
Craft scissors or wire cutters
Floral picks
Floral pins
Floral tape

Please familiarize yourself with basic techniques found in General Instructions, pg. 108, before beginning project. The measurements on the Placement Diagram indicate the length of the stem from the base of the flower or lowest leaf.

INSTRUCTIONS

1. Refer to Placement Diagram, page 103, for measurements and follow Preparing Flowers and Greenery, pg. 108, to separate, trim, and wrap stems of all flowers and greenery. Use floral tape to wrap three willow stem clusters together. Trim wrapped cluster to 13". Repeat with remaining willow stem clusters.

2. Insert handle of bouquet holder through center of bouquet collar; glue in place.

3. Refer to Placement Diagram to insert large roses, rosebuds, lilacs, bayberry clusters, tiny berry clusters, and willow stems into bouquet holder.

4. Cut four 6" lengths of 1"w striped ribbon. Match raw edges of one length to form loop; secure ends by wrapping with thread. Repeat with remaining lengths. Refer to Assembling Bouquets, pg. 109, to insert floral pin into each ribbon loop. Insert floral-pinned loops into bouquet holder.

5. Insert leaves into bouquet.

6. To make colored bow, measure to a starting point 14" from one end of ⅞"w ribbon and hold ribbon at this point between thumb and forefinger. For first loop, measure 13" from starting point and fold ribbon to form a loop by matching starting point and second point. Measure 13" from second point and form loop by matching second point and third point. Leave a 14" length of

ribbon at the end of the second loop for streamer. Hand baste all loops and streamers together at the base of loops. Pull basting thread as tight as possible; secure and clip thread.

7. Hand sew one end of remaining striped ribbon to center of colored bow.

8. Matching raw edges, fold picot-edge ribbon in half. Matching centers, hand sew fold of picot-edge ribbon to colored bow on top of striped ribbon.

9. Refer to Assembling Bouquets, pg. 109, to insert floral pin into bow. Insert floral-pinned bow into bouquet holder.

PLACEMENT DIAGRAM

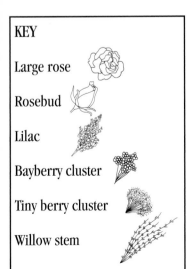

KEY

Large rose

Rosebud

Lilac

Bayberry cluster

Tiny berry cluster

Willow stem

BRIDESMAID'S BOUQUET

SUPPLIES

1⅜" x 3½" bouquet holder
6½" dia. lace bouquet collar
1 yd — 6"w colored tulle
2¼ yds — 1½"w colored satin ribbon
1¼ yds — 1½"w striped picot-edge
    wired ribbon
5 colored silk roses with leaves
2 colored silk rosebuds with leaves
3 large white filler sprays
2 large colored filler sprays
6 large colored fluffy sprays
Hot glue gun and glue sticks
    (optional)
Thick, clear-drying craft glue
Craft scissors or wire cutters
Floral picks
Floral pins
Floral tape

Please familiarize yourself with basic techniques found in General Instructions, pg. 108, before beginning project. The measurements on the Placement Diagram indicate the length of the stem from the base of the flower or lowest leaf.

INSTRUCTIONS

1. Refer to Placement Diagram, pg. 105, for measurements and follow Preparing Flowers and Greenery, pg. 108, to separate, trim, and wrap stems of all flowers.

2. Insert handle of bouquet holder through center of bouquet collar; glue in place.

3. Refer to Placement Diagram, pg. 105, to insert roses, rosebuds, two white filler sprays, colored filler sprays, and five fluffy sprays into bouquet holder.

4. For ribbon loops, cut two 8" lengths of 1½"w colored ribbon and two 8" lengths of 1½"w striped ribbon. Matching raw edges, fold one length in half to form a loop; secure ends by wrapping with thread. Repeat with remaining lengths of ribbon. Refer to Assembling Bouquets, pg. 109, to inset floral pin through each ribbon loop. Insert floral-pinned loops into bouquet holder.

5. To make tulle loops, cut four 9" lengths of tulle. Matching short edges, fold one length in half. Baste ¼" from short edges.

Tightly gather ends (Fig. 126); secure and clip thread. Repeat with remaining lengths of tulle. Refer to Assembling Bouquets, pg. 109, to insert floral pin through each tulle loop. Insert floral-pinned loops into bouquet holder.

Fig. 126

6. To make bow, measure to a starting point 17" from one end of colored ribbon and hold ribbon at this point between thumb and forefinger. For first loop, measure 14" from starting point and fold ribbon to form a loop by matching starting point and second point. Measure 17" from second point and form loop by matching second point and third point. Leave a 15" length of ribbon at the end of the second loop for streamer. Hand baste all loops and streamers together at the base of loops. Pull basting thread as tight as possible; secure and clip thread.

7. For striped streamers, measure 16" from one end of striped ribbon. Fold ribbon at this point. Gather by wrapping with thread; secure and clip thread. Hand sew gathered fold to center of colored bow. Refer to Assembling Bouquets, pg. 109, to insert floral pin through bow.

8. Insert floral-pinned bow into bouquet holder.

9. Following Preparing Flowers and Greenery, pg. 108, separate and wrap leaves from roses and cuttings from remaining filler spray and fluffy spray. To fill in bouquet, insert leaves and cuttings into bouquet holder.

PLACEMENT DIAGRAM

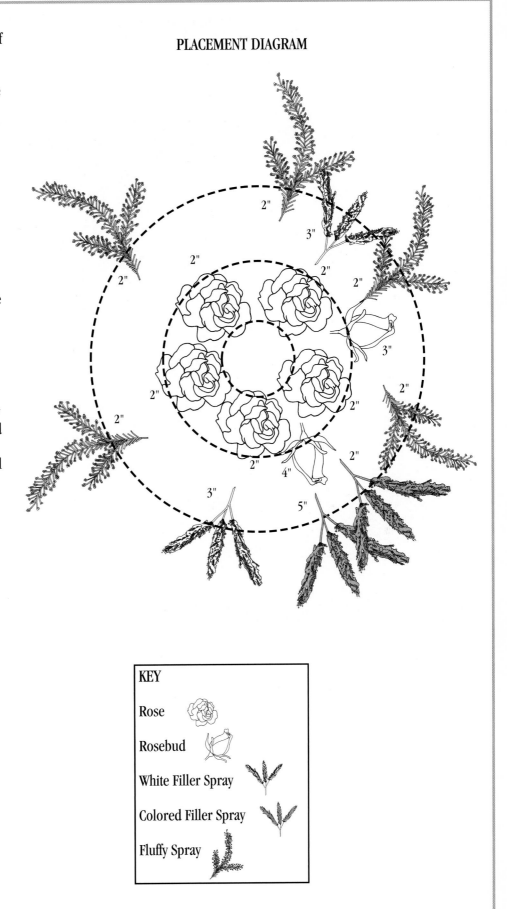

KEY

Rose

Rosebud

White Filler Spray

Colored Filler Spray

Fluffy Spray

105

BRIDESMAID'S SHOES

SUPPLIES

1 pair dyed satin shoes
1 pair shoe clips
¾ yd — 1½"w striped picot-edge
   wired ribbon
2 small colored silk rosebuds
2 — 2½" pieces of colored filler
   spray
Hot glue gun and glue sticks

INSTRUCTIONS

1. Cut ribbon in half. Tie each
   ribbon length in a bow. Hand sew
   one bow to each shoe clip. Refer
   to Fig. 127 to fold and notch
   ribbon ends.

Fig. 127

2. Glue one rosebud and one filler
   spray to center of each bow. Clip
   to toes of shoes.

RICE BAG

SUPPLIES

(*Note*: *Supplies are for making one rice bag.*)

  10" square of colored tulle
  ½ yd — 2¼"w colored double-face satin ribbon
  ⅛ yd — 1"w white wired ribbon
  ¼ yd — ¼"w colored satin ribbon
  4" — ⅛"w colored satin ribbon
  1½" piece of filler spray
  Hot glue gun and glue sticks
  Tracing paper
  2 tablespoons rice or birdseed

INSTRUCTIONS

1. For circle pattern, fold tracing paper in half and place folded edge along heavy solid line on pattern (shown in dark grey on page 112). Use a pencil to trace pattern on tracing paper; cut out traced pattern. Unfold pattern and lay it flat. Cut out tulle circle.

2. Matching raw edges, fold 2¼"w ribbon in half; lightly crease center. Unfold ribbon. Place ribbon on work surface. Fold each short edge to center, overlapping center crease by ½"; pin in place. Hand baste across center of ribbon, stitching through all layers. Pull basting thread as tight as possible to gather ribbon; secure and clip thread. Tie ⅛"w ribbon in a knot over gathering line; trim ends of ⅛"w ribbon close to knot.

3. Place ribbon on work surface with overlapped edges and ribbon knot facing up. Center tulle circle on top of ribbon.

4. Pour rice into center of tulle circle. Gather tulle and ribbon around rice. Use ¼"w ribbon to tie a bow around gathered tulle and ribbon right above rice. Trim ¼"w ribbon ends as desired.

5. For rosette, hand baste ¼" from one long edge of wired ribbon. Pull basting thread as tight as possible; secure and clip thread. Fold one short edge of length at a 45° angle *(Fig. 128)*; hand sew bottom edges together. For center of rosette, keep edges even and turn point of ribbon to inside as shown in Fig. 129; hand sew edges together. Continue turning center of rosette to inside and hand sewing edges together. At end of ribbon, fold remaining raw edge to back of rosette at a 45° angle; hand sew in place. Secure and clip thread.

Fig. 128

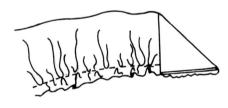

Fig. 129

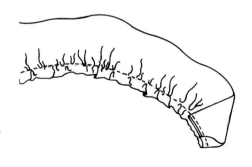

6. Glue filler spray and rosette above bow.

CORSAGE

SUPPLIES

  ⅔ yd — 1½"w striped picot-edge wired ribbon
  6" — ⅛"w white satin ribbon
  Large colored silk rose with leaf cluster
  2 — 7½" pieces of fern
  2 pearl sprays
  Corsage pin
  Hot glue gun and glue sticks
  Craft scissors or wire cutters
  Floral tape

INSTRUCTIONS

1. Separate leaf cluster from rose stem. Trim stem of rose to 4". Holding rose, leaf cluster, and fern pieces together and beginning just below rose blossom, wrap stems together with floral tape, continuing to end of rose stem. Twist stem around pencil.

2. Glue pearl sprays to stems behind rose.

3. Tie striped ribbon in a bow. Tie ⅛"w ribbon in a knot around center of bow, placing knot on wrong side. Tie ⅛"w ribbon in a knot around stems. Glue knot to back of stems. Trim ⅛"w ribbon ends close to knot.

4. Refer to Fig. 130 to fold and notch striped ribbon ends.

Fig. 130

General Instructions

PREPARING FLOWERS AND GREENERY

Flowers and greenery may be purchased singly or grouped together on a stem (a spray). To best utilize a spray, cut each stem off where it joins the main stem. Individual stems should be wrapped with floral tape. Floral tape is available in white, green, and brown. To use floral tape, stretch tape slightly while wrapping it around stem. This stretching action releases the tape's adhesive and allows the tape to stick to the stem and to itself.

If a flower stem is not long enough or the stem is too flimsy, a floral pick can be added. If a flower stem is too flimsy, another option is to add a wire stem.

Flowers and/or greenery may be joined together with floral tape before inserting them into the arrangement or bouquet. Wrap **each** stem with floral tape. Holding all stems together, join stems by wrapping with floral tape.

Adding a Floral Pick

Floral picks are small wooden stakes with thin wire attached. To attach floral pick, place pick alongside stem no less than 1" from end of stem. Wrap wire around stem and pick. Starting at base of flower, begin wrapping stem with floral tape. Continue wrapping floral tape around stem and pick until end of pick is reached *(Fig. 131)*.

Fig. 131

Floral picks can be added to pearl loops, pearl stems, and any other floral arrangement or bouquet part that has a stem that can be wrapped with the floral pick wire.

Adding a Wire Stem

Floral wire is available in a variety of sizes; 20 gauge is a medium size wire and should be suitable for most flowers and greenery. To attach floral wire to flowers, heat one end of the wire and pass it through the plastic base of the flower as shown in Fig. 132. Bend both ends of wire down close to stem. Wrap stem and wire with floral tape; continue wrapping until end of wire is reached.

Fig. 132

To add floral wire to greenery, loop one end of the wire around stem of the greenery (Fig. 133). Pinch loop closed with needle nose pliers. Wrap loop, stem, and wire with floral tape; continue wrapping until end of wire is reached.

Fig. 133

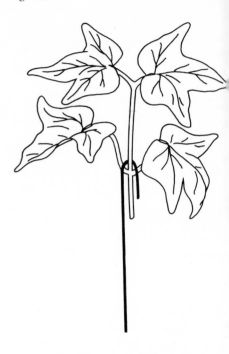

ASSEMBLING ARRANGEMENTS

Trim and wrap flowers and greenery before inserting them into foam. Dip each stem into thick, clear-drying craft glue before inserting it into foam. Insert each stem approximately 1" into foam.

Floral pins can be used to hold flowers and greenery in place. Dip floral pin into thick, clear-drying craft glue and place pin over flower stem or greenery stem. Insert pin into foam. Floral pins should also be inserted through ribbon bows and pearl loops. A hot glue gun and glue sticks may be helpful in assembling the floral arrangement because of its quick set-up time. It should be used with care because the hot glue gun can melt plastic and foam.

If after inserting all flowers, there are empty spaces in the floral arrangement, fill in those spots with leaves, smaller flowers, or pearl stems as desired.

ASSEMBLING BOUQUETS

ach project (except Satin Sophisticate ride's Bouquet) has a diagram for ower placement. Fig. 134 shows a acement Diagram, which represents the eas of a bouquet holder. Fig. 135 shows tual placement of flowers. Refer to g. 134 and Fig. 135 for the following: e inner circle (A) shows where flowers e to be placed in foam within center ng of bouquet holder, the middle circle) shows where flowers are to be placed foam within the outer ring of bouquet lder at an angle to foam, and the outer rcle (C) shows where flowers are to be aced straight into the sides of bouquet lder.

3. 134

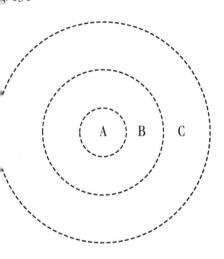

Fig. 135

When assembling your bouquet, it is helpful to stand the bouquet holder upright in a bottle. Fill bottom of bottle with sand to stabilize bottle. Trim and wrap flowers, greenery, and pearl loops before inserting them into foam of bouquet holder. Dip each stem into thick, clear-drying craft glue before inserting into foam. Insert each stem approximately 1" into foam.

Floral pins can be used to hold flowers and greenery in place. Dip floral pin into thick, clear-drying craft glue and place pin over flower stem or greenery stem. Insert pin into foam of bouquet holder. Floral pins should also be inserted through ribbon or fabric roses/rosettes, ribbon bows or loops, pearl loops, and gathered doilies. A hot glue gun and glue sticks may be helpful in assembling the bouquet because of its quick set-up time. It should be used with care because the hot glue can melt plastic and foam. If after inserting all flowers, there are empty spaces in the bouquet, fill in those spots with leaves, smaller flowers, or ribbon loops as desired. After all ribbons have been placed in bouquet, refer to Fig. 136 to fold and notch ribbon ends.

Fig. 136

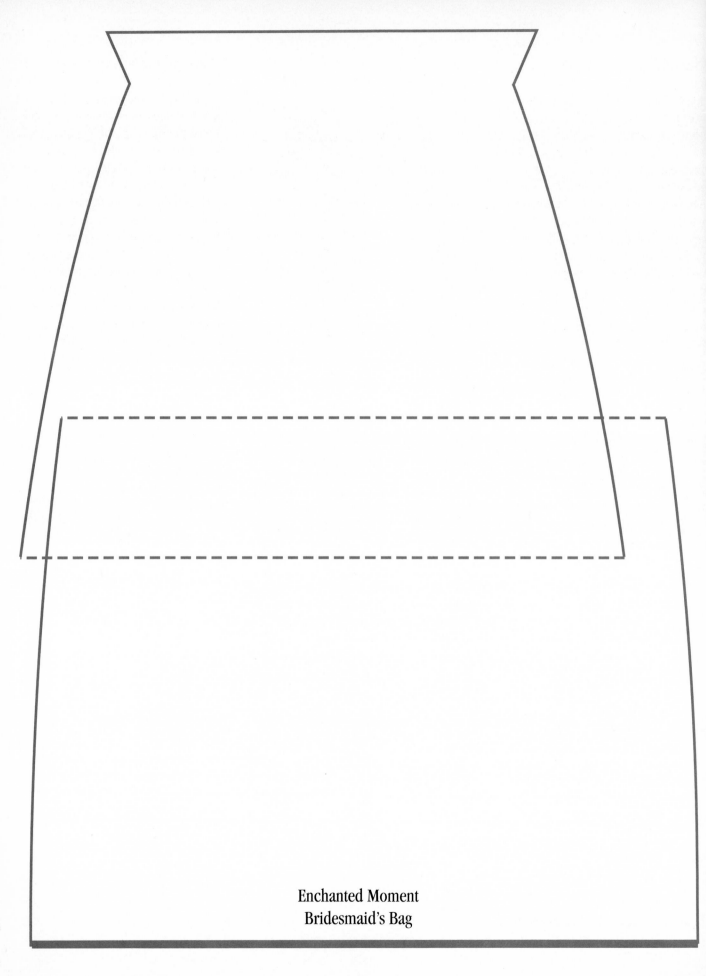

Enchanted Moment
Bridesmaid's Bag

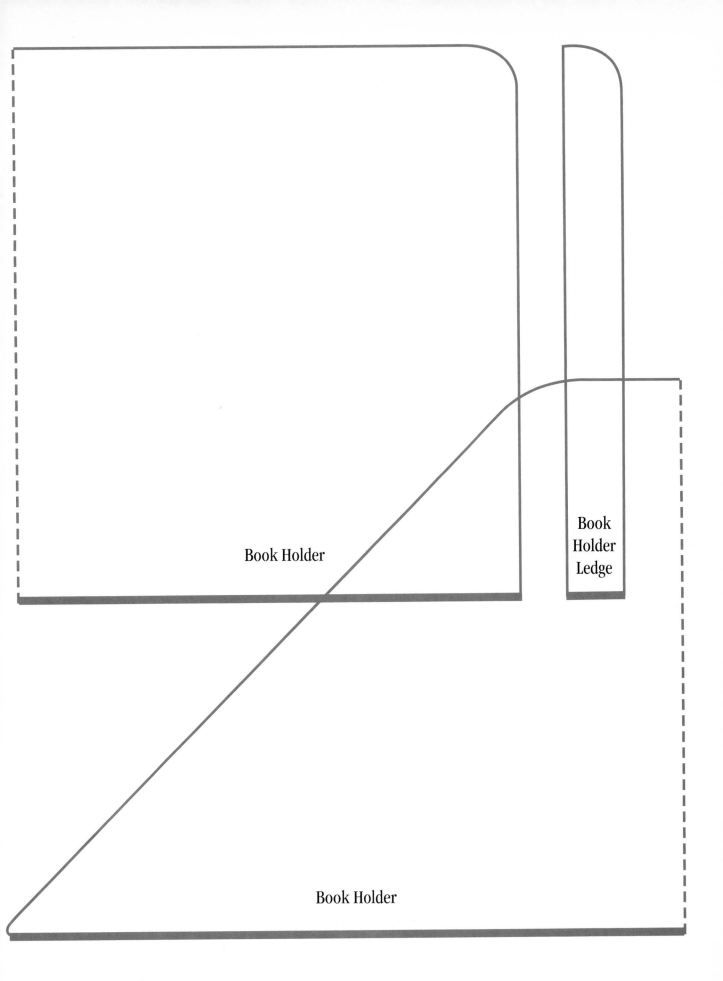

Book Holder

Book
Holder
Ledge

Book Holder

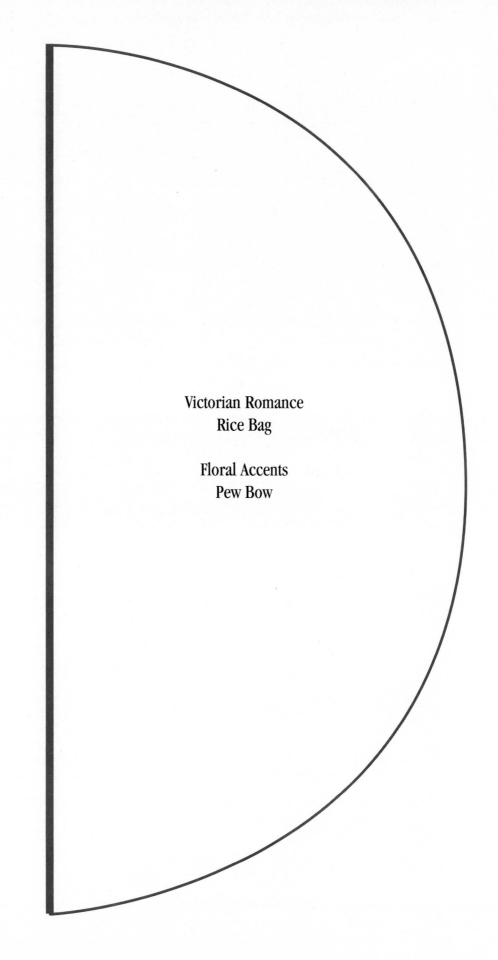

Victorian Romance
Rice Bag

Floral Accents
Pew Bow